NO DUMB QUESTIONS

For the 92%ers

—*Jason and Travis*

NO DUMB QUESTIONS

AND ALL OF OUR ^DUMBEST ANSWERS

JASON & TRAVIS KELCE

wm

WILLIAM MORROW
An Imprint of HarperCollins*Publishers*

NO DUMB QUESTIONS. Copyright © 2026 by Wondery LLC. All rights reserved. Printed in the United Kingdom. No part of this book may be used or reproduced in any manner whatsoever without written permission except in the case of brief quotations embodied in critical articles and reviews. For information, address HarperCollins Publishers, 195 Broadway, New York, NY 10007. In Europe, HarperCollins Publishers, Macken House, 39/40 Mayor Street Upper, Dublin 1, D01 C9W8, Ireland.

HarperCollins books may be purchased for educational, business, or sales promotional use. For information, please email the Special Markets Department at SPsales@harpercollins.com.

hc.com

FIRST EDITION

Designed by Nancy Singer
Illustrations by Lukas Bischoff

Additional illustrations: harmonica©MDSAJJADHOSSAN/stock.adobe.com; darts©Yada/stock.adobe.com; hockey stick and puck©Ornavi/stock.adobe.com; sparkler©cac_tus/stock.adobe.com; candy bar©Mari Bryk/stock.adobe.com; apples©Vectorial Arts/stock.adobe.com; football©asgraphics13/stock.adobe.com; Motorcycle©Michael Hinkle/stock.adobe.com; ice skate©trianatio/stock.adobe.com; Boot©David/stock.adobe.com; cereal box©supplement/stock.adobe.com; boxing gloves©NK/stock.adobe.com; steak, beer mug, taco©Mariia Mazaeva/stock.adobe.com; rugby ball©bima saputra/stock.adobe.com; gorilla©marinavorona/stock.adobe.com; pineapple©b.illustrations/stock.adobe.com

Endpaper illustrations: Travis and Jason by Lukas Bischoff; football©asgraphics13/stock.adobe.com; microphone©Irina Popovfootball©asgraphics13/stock.adobe.com

Library of Congress Cataloging-in-Publication Data has been applied for.

ISBN 978-0-06-348957-8

26 27 28 29 CPI 10 9 8 7 6 5 4 3 2

Contents

Introduction

Spoiler alert. You're about to read a book that was written by two people who both got kicked out of preschool. Let that sink in . . .

How old are you in preschool anyway? Three? Four? Dad was right to question why I was given a spork in the first place. But a kid and I were playing at a cafeteria table and for some reason, we were stabbing each other with our sporks. We thought it was funny, as any red-blooded little boy would when dealing with a utensil anomaly, limited supervision, and a willing accomplice. But as even the best-laid plans often do—which I'm obviously not saying this was—it went off the rails. I got him good enough that the next day his dad was bringing him into school with four little spork dots smack in the middle of his forehead. And I was promptly kicked out of preschool after copping to my participation in our unauthorized sporking contest.

Dad's response was "Why weren't you watching him?" Like they handed me a spork and unleashed me into the wild. This was obviously not going to go down as a Kelce's fault on Ed's watch. And based on personal firsthand experience of playtime with me gone wrong, Travis's summary alludes to a little more intention than I recall. "They were playing; Jason didn't like how they were playing; so he stabbed him in the face with a spork. That's what happened."

But at the end of the day, Spork Kid's dad was just not having it. Even though his son was partaking as well. His son just didn't win—if there's even a winner here. But now that kid will never learn, since they removed his best competition by kicking my four-year-old butt out of there. He'll be getting sporked for the rest of his life.

We've briefly talked about trying to find Spork Kid to come on the podcast—see how he's fared in life, get his version of events—but we haven't gone down that road yet. I feel like sporks aren't even really around anymore, or at least not as readily available today as they apparently were back then.

But I chock this story up to doing my part to add to the Kelce lore— stories that are all now very well-documented thanks to the *New Heights* podcast.

Because of that podcast I'm sitting here cowriting an introduction to a freaking book, and it's just another "What the fuck is going on?" moment in a long line of surreal moments that seem to keep happening. The ones that make you sit up and pay attention to the complete absurdity of your life. Per usual, we have no business doing any of this. But it's amazing what can happen when you don't take yourself too seriously.

I do think the "What the fuck is going on?" question is fair though. I wasn't even supposed to have the playing career I did. Thirteen years, seven Pro Bowls, and a Super Bowl win with the Eagles. And who would have thought I'd have more Emmy nominations than Super Bowl rings? Not-fucking-me, that's who. I was a walk-on in college, earning my scholarship after my freshman year, a sixth-round draft pick in the NFL. And in the spirit of "No Dumb Questions," I'll preemptively tell you that there are only seven rounds in the NFL Draft.

"Jason Kelce is too small." That was the most pervasive narrative, which is one I made sure to reference in my speech during the Eagles' Super Bowl parade in 2018. Even then, I saw the value in taking control of my own narrative. People always have a lot to say. But it's always better when you can tell your own story.

It's one of the reasons we started a podcast in the first place. Having a direct and unfiltered conversation with the fans was enticing. Was it a dumb idea? Probably. But sometimes the dumbest ideas are the best ones, because sometimes they lead to something magical that no one else is dumb enough to think of or crazy enough to try.

Like how we started the podcast when we were both still playing. When you win, you're on top of the world, but damn, tapping in after a loss requires a whole other level of brutal honesty and reflection. It doesn't get more real than being the fly on the wall during those conversations. But the silver lining is getting to have those conversations with someone who gets it, someone who's living it, too, who just happens to be your little brother. And conversations with your brother will always be authentic as shit. Because they know it all and have seen it all and are always game to call you out on your bullshit. But outside the lens of the media or the "experts," and before my day job was being one of those "experts," *New Heights* was a way we could talk about whatever we want, say whatever we want, and talk to whomever we want. I mean, shout-out to whoever sat in a room with Trav and me, hearing us bitch and bond over football, family, and life, and thought, "I'd listen to that."

But here we are!

At the end of the day, I get to do this with my best friend on the planet. Everyone gets to see the guy we've seen all these years up close—the human exclamation point. Taylor really nailed it with that description. And I get to talk ball and life with my brother every week, and people actually want to hear what we have to say. Just another "What the fuck is going on?" moment to add to the list.

My girls are holding strong and not following in the Kelce preschool expulsion tradition . . . so far, anyways. I'll give Kylie's genes the credit for that, since apparently, they don't get the credit for anything in the looks department.

TRAVIS: LITTLE BROTHER

In classic little-brother fashion, I also got kicked out of preschool just like my big bro before me.

I can't believe Jason says he had never heard this one.

I was playing checkers.

And I was winning. Because I don't fucking lose at checkers.

And if you win, you stay on—that's the thing. That's the Kelce way. So, I keep winning and keep winning, and the teacher goes, "You know, Travis, you have to share." But I had my foolproof argument ready. "That's not how this works." Dad always taught us, "If you win, you stay on—winners stay on."

When Jason heard this story after I recounted it on *New Heights*, he countered, "Well, it's kind of hard to win, Travis, IF YOU NEVER MOVE YOUR BACK ROW." But obviously that was just my elite strategy as a four-year-old checkers prodigy.

"No. You have to share."

But I was holding my ground. "No, I don't." And I took the chair I was sitting on and launched it in her direction. It's preschool, so this is one of those pint-size plastic chairs. But still, I followed in my big brother's foot-steps getting booted from preschool.

Sorry, Mom.

But honestly, I've followed in his footsteps since birth.

Growing up in Cleveland Heights, Jason and I had the best damn child-hood. The traditional Midwest, backyard ball, don't-come-home-until-the-streetlights-come-on kind of childhood. We did almost everything together. Inventing games and winning imaginary Super Bowls years be-fore we'd win the real thing. We made everything a competition. We'd get called in from playing outside and promptly start playing cards inside. Whatever it was—basketball, home run derbies, and yes, even checkers, and always with a dare that would usually end in parental intervention. I dared Jason to try and throw a football over our three-story house. One broken window later, we found out he couldn't.

Fast-forward: We're still those kids. Grown-ass kids living the dream, just like we were back then. Now with real Super Bowl rings and aspirations of turning pro realized, creating *New Heights* was a way for us to tap into that nostalgia all over again and live out those childhood football dreams together. We would go months during the season, each with his own crazy schedule, never having time to catch up, and we made it everyone's problem by rectifying that with a podcast. But who wouldn't want to talk to the Big Guy on the regular?

People didn't always know we were brothers aside from the name on the backs of our jerseys. We were so different to the people looking in, and not just because of Jason's love for cutoffs and flip-flops in the winter. Or my animated personality on the field compared to Jason's more cerebral approach. But now our similarities, brotherly bond, and family values are on full display every week. *New Heights* has given people a glimpse into what everyone close to us has always known—we're best friends and actually more alike than you would ever think.

We also get to talk about football. And I fucking love football. Being in the NFL and playing on the biggest stage will always be the coolest thing in the world to me.

But if you don't know football, or if you just gotta ask, we created "No Dumb Questions" as your safe place for all those burning ones you think are too dumb to ask anyone other than us, apparently. I can't promise our answers are life-changing or even close to accurate, but we got you covered. I've always said acting like you're the smartest one in the room is just not the way to go. There's always something to learn.

We're always down to soak up the knowledge from people around us and lean into learning new things. Like friend of the show Will Ferrell said, you got to "full send." From those days growing up on Coleridge Road to now, we've always been full send in anything we do.

Now we got a book—plot twist for the guy who claims he can't read well. And I get to hang with my big brother every week on *New Heights*—where we're talking about the game we love, turning into little kids chopping it up with our childhood heroes and some of the coolest people on earth, and we have all our family and friends along for the ride.

Honestly, we're just two brothers from Cleveland who are still wrapping our heads around living our dreams on and off the field. But manifestation, baby, it's a beautiful thing.

Alright nah.

PART 1

FAMILY

1

Brotherhood, Childhood, and Kelce Family Lore

What are your favorite pranks to pull as a middle-school-age boy?

92%er: Willow from South Carolina via the Heights Hotline

JASON: Thank you so much. Willow, let me tell you about a game called poop dollar, all right? Here's what you're going to want to do.

TRAVIS: Poop dollar is a *great one.*

JASON: You're going to want to get . . . they're middle school. I feel like a dollar works still for a middle schooler, right?

TRAVIS: What? One hundred percent.

JASON: Yeah. Take a dollar.

TRAVIS: A $5 would get them excited, but they actually still might keep the dollar.

JASON: If you really want to, like, really get them, $20 bill, that will for sure work.

TRAVIS: It's going to take some dirty work, though, so you want to go get some hospital gloves.

JASON: Get some gloves. Glove up for this. Hopefully, you have a pet. That's the easiest-case scenario.

TRAVIS: Makes it way easier, but if not, just go to the park.

JASON: Yeah, or you can do it yourself, but . . .

TRAVIS: We've never gone that far.

JASON: I'm gonna guess . . . yeah, we haven't done that yet. You're gonna want to take a $20 bill, fold it in, like, a U-shape. Roam your backyard for some type of dropping of, uh, excrement of some kind. Take the U-shape so the *bill only*—

TRAVIS: Bill only!

JASON: Not your hand. Bill only.

TRAVIS: But you got gloves just in case.

JASON: You smush it right in the middle of the bill. Now you have it in the middle of the bill. Fold that puppy over on top of each other. Set it down where the boys are gonna be. You know they're gonna wander by.

TRAVIS: They're gonna pass by. It's gonna be enticing. You gotta be around, though. So you gotta camp out. You gotta hide out. You have to be there while they pick it up, or you're not gonna be as satisfied.

JASON: Yes. And you're gonna want to leave it so that they discover it, pick it up, and then find out that, lo and behold, there's poop inside of it.

TRAVIS: And you scream:

JASON and TRAVIS: POOP DOLLAAAA!!

JASON: So that'll work. That's a good one. That's a great one for middle school boys, or really boys of any age.

TRAVIS: Yeah. Men, grown men. That gets them too. I would say another one that we knew about, that we didn't really partake in as much, but Icy Hot in the jockstrap always works. So you can go Icy Hot in the . . . it's kind of cruel, but it takes about an hour to wear off.

JASON: Chris Pessic got me in ice hockey.

TRAVIS: There you go.

JASON: Remember Chris?

TRAVIS: Yeah, of course I do.

JASON: So the freshmen used to have to unload the buses or something like that, and we had a loss or something, and I was trying to get the hell out of there. Didn't unload the bus, came back the next day, put my jockstrap on, went out on the ice. Not a fun day.

TRAVIS: Yeah, both icy and hot . . .

JASON: Nothing icy about it, it was pure hot. There's zero ice to it.

TRAVIS: Yeah, it can feel a little cruel, and if they don't wear jockstraps just the boxers work.

JASON: Yep.

TRAVIS: Boxers work just as good.

JASON: Yeah, I mean, I wouldn't do that. That's too far to me, Willow, but what are some other good ones? We're just not great pranksters.

TRAVIS: We didn't do a lot of pranking.

JASON: If you have one of those like hoses on the sink, put a little rubber band

---

around that so that when they turn the faucet on, it just sprays them right in the face. It's a good one. What are some other good pranks?

TRAVIS: You can booby-trap them. You can always booby-trap them, get a balloon full of whipped cream or something like that. They open a door, all of a sudden smacks them right in the face. That takes some good work, you got to be kind of handy.

JASON: Where's [Willow] from? South Carolina? Are there alligators in South Carolina?

TRAVIS: I'm sure they ventured up there.

JASON: I mean, if it's a pool day, get an alligator, duct-tape its mouth closed, and throw it in the pool.

TRAVIS: Yeah, well, good luck with that.

JASON: They're not that strong at opening their mouth, they're only strong closing it, so duct tape will hold it, you'll be good.

TRAVIS: Yeah, that sounds terrifying.

JASON: It'll be very scary, though.

TRAVIS: Yeah. They will hate you forever. Please let us know what you ended up doing. We can't wait to hear what you go with!

Between Travis and Jason, who lifts the heaviest weights in the weight room?

92%er: Jared Brown via email

TRAVIS: This might be the dumbest question I've ever gotten asked in my life.

JASON: Everybody saw that commercial with Chunkies Campbell and you beat me in an arm wrestling match.

THIS MIGHT BE THE DUMBEST QUESTION I'VE EVER GOTTEN ASKED IN MY LIFE.

TRAVIS: Yeah. *[flexing]* Who wants the champ? Who benches the most and squats the most? Well, I don't bench or squat, so it looks like Jason wins both of those events. And he's clearly stronger than me, probably close to twice as strong as me. And to be honest, man, your ten-yard start still might be faster than mine.

JASON: I don't know.

TRAVIS: I remember we raced one time in college and you fucking got me. And I was like, this doesn't make any fucking sense. He's forty pounds heavier than me and he's quicker than me.

JASON: I had a good start. Good start.

TRAVIS: This guy is on the juice. That's what I thought of you, Jason.

JASON: And then you saw me take my shirt off and you're like, this guy is not on the juice. When's the last time you back-squatted?

TRAVIS: I'll do the Keiser squat, work more explosion and all of that instead of just getting under a squat bar.

JASON: You do it for the functionality of being an athlete, not so much for the strength purposes.

TRAVIS: Yeah, get everything firing.

JASON: What about bench?

TRAVIS: What are you throwing up?

JASON: I don't know. And I always before every season, I want to squat over five hundred pounds just to mentally feel like I'm still strong. I want to say the most I've done in the last like four years was something like 575.

TRAVIS: My bones just rattled when you said that.

JASON: In season, I like to try and still squat heavy because I feel like it helps me keep my strength. Benching heavy . . . I mean, I still bench. In the off-season, I'll hit 150s on the dumbbells.

TRAVIS: I was about to say, where the fuck are you going with this? Dumbbells? Nice.

JASON: Yeah, dumbbell bench 150. I don't really try and max out on bench press just because I've seen so many guys tear their pecs trying to do that.

TRAVIS: That's terrifying.

JASON: I don't think having a really good bench press necessarily benefits playing football that much. Like I think there's a point of diminished returns in that regard.

TRAVIS: Yeah, I'm with you on that. I don't bench one bit. I get everything firing. These shoulders are fucked. So there's only so much I can do.

JASON: You figure out what you can still do and what you can't. You know what I mean? There's certain things I just don't even do anymore because it bothers my back or bothers my knee. And I know it's going to bother me, like single leg squats now already. What are those, Bulgarians? I know that if I do that, weighted-up there, my knees are going to be sore the next day. So you figure a way to get that done without loading it up too-too heavy.

TRAVIS: Yeah, I'm with you on that.

Can Jason tell us more about his musical background? Does he think he'll pick it back up now that he's retired?

92%er: mwags75 via Club 92

JASON: Pick it back up? What are they talking about?

TRAVIS: Jason has never not been musically gifted.

JASON: I got two hot-selling Christmas albums back-to-back years. What are these people talking about? "Pick it back up"?!

TRAVIS: This guy is selling vinyls. What do you mean, pick it back up?

JASON: In Cleveland Heights, everybody had to start with an instrument in fourth grade.

TRAVIS: "Hot Cross Buns." Oh no, you're talking about a real instrument. A recorder.

JASON: Well, no, you started an instrument too. You played "Hot Cross Buns" on a trumpet for a little bit.

TRAVIS: The recorder.

JASON: You gave it up quick. You got over it very quickly.

TRAVIS: Everybody wants to play the drums, I feel like—the percussion.

JASON: You would have been a good drummer.

TRAVIS: I would have been drumming the fuck out of that thing. But no, I got forced to play something else. You had already picked the coolest of the horns in the saxophone, and I didn't want to be like you, so I chose something else, and I picked the little fucking—

JASON: Miles Davis might think differently.

TRAVIS: The little Sammy Davis, no, not Sammy Davis Jr. Is it? No . . . Louis Armstrong.

JASON: Who are you thinking of? Are you thinking of a trumpet player?

TRAVIS: Louis Armstrong.

JASON: If you're talking about cool, though, you can't leave out Miles Davis. *Birth of the Cool.* So yeah, Travis picked up trumpet and got out of that fairly quickly. Did you do it in middle school or did you—?

TRAVIS: Only in middle school.

JASON: When did you stop?

TRAVIS: I stopped in eighth grade. You only had to do it for sixth and seventh, I think.

JASON: I started with saxophone and played it all the way through high school. I played in symphonic band in high school as well and I played in the jazz ensemble, which at Cleveland Heights was pretty prestigious, let me tell you.

TRAVIS: Yeah, that was pretty sweet. I used to love going to those. The orchestra ones were cool. When it was the jazz ensemble, I was all in on that.

JASON: Those are the cool cats.

TRAVIS: I'll show up for this one. Watch Jason step up and fucking just rip a solo.

JASON: Rip a baritone sax solo.

TRAVIS: Electric.

JASON: Mr. Baker was the band director as well as the jazz ensemble director. And man, I tell people this all the time. I really think playing band and playing music in general has allowed me to excel in sport and other things, because as with anything, I encourage kids to play as many sports, do as many extracurriculars as you can that you enjoy. Because you end up drawing things from each one of those that is unique and different.

TRAVIS: One thousand percent, yeah.

JASON: With band, in my opinion, if you want to learn the importance and the value of practice, nothing will teach you that more clear than an instrument.

TRAVIS: Practice.

JASON: The first time you pick up that instrument and try to play anything, you are going to be terrible. But the more you practice at it, you will get good. Like it's that simple. It's just so right in your face how much that affects how you play.

You also learn to tempo how you learn. So when you're learning a song, if you try and play at full speed, you can't do it right away. So what do you do? You slow it down. You walk through it, you go through the fingerings, you go through the notes, and you do the same thing in football. When you're going with a route, if you just try and run at full speed every single time, no, there's a time to utilize tempo. There's a time to walk through it and hit every step.

TRAVIS: Technique.

JASON: Yeah, so I think that there's a lot of carryover in band and a lot of things that people try and do, and it's a lot of fun. And I had a really, really good teacher that I've kept in touch with throughout the years, and Brett Baker, it wouldn't have been right to not thank him [in a recent speech].

TRAVIS: Yeah, I hear you on that.

JASON: Because he taught me a lot.

TRAVIS: I'll tell you what, I was never in music, but I always felt like Mr. Baker was kind of like, hovering, looking over me because I was your little brother.

JASON: Well, he was. Because Mr. Baker was a big football fan.

TRAVIS: That too, yeah.

JASON: He loved football. He played football. Maybe that's why I connected with him so much.

TRAVIS: He's always been a family friend, yeah, for sure.

JASON: He's a Steelers fan, which we don't hold that against him too much, but—

TRAVIS: I mean, you were a big Jerome Bettis fan growing up, so—

JASON: Yeah, that's true. Very true.

TRAVIS: But who wasn't? That's the fucking Bus. I mean, Jason, you picked up a lot of different instruments, too.

JASON: Well, in jazz ensemble, I had to play saxophone, and then on certain songs, you would transition to a bass clarinet. And in jazz lab, I started playing trombone for a couple years.

TRAVIS: What?

JASON: Maybe one year. Yeah, I mean, I wasn't . . . I could not do it again if I tried. I don't remember any of the notes or anything, but it was just fun to mess around with that. So I like trying new instruments. You know, since I've been out of band in high school, I've taught myself how to play guitar. I've tried harmonica, which, dude, little Blues Traveler. I can't do that. I would love to get to that point.

TRAVIS: Big Don, Big Uncle Don was a harmonica [player]. You remember that?

JASON: Was he?

TRAVIS: Dude, you don't remember him?

JASON: I do not.

TRAVIS: What?! I think he got one of us a harmonica for like our birthday or Christmas.

JASON: I vaguely remember that.

TRAVIS: And we had it around the house. We never really actually played it.

JASON: I think instruments are fun to try and pick up and learn how to play. And then you kind of fall into which ones you really like. And I always wish I would have taken piano more seriously, because that's . . . it's always nice when a piano is there and you can just sit down and start playing the keys.

TRAVIS: It's impressive. It's impressive. I wish . . . because that's actually where I started in music in elementary school.

JASON: I know!

TRAVIS: Dad used to throw me in the piano lessons and I got decent. I remember going to my first recital and hearing everyone clap for me because I'm a little fucking kid and I just finished a song. But it was so rewarding. I was just like, man, I like this feeling. I want to do this more. And then I picked up a football and that was that. Thank you. Thank you, mwags, for the question. And Jason is going to go for yet another top-of-the-charts Christmas album again next year.

JASON: We're doing it again.

TRAVIS: You got to keep that thing going, man.

JASON: Why not? It's a blast to put together.

Was Mama Kelce a sports fan before having her boys?

92%er: @leighannellis5748 via YouTube

MAMA KELCE: Yes, I was.

TRAVIS: Niiiiice!

MAMA KELCE: I was a sports fan.

TRAVIS: East side of Cleveland, how could you not?

MAMA KELCE: When I was in school, there was no Title IX. Really didn't have collegiate sports for women, about the only thing you could do was be in the Olympics.

JASON: Well, they had them, but there weren't as many opportunities.

MAMA KELCE: No, there weren't a lot of opportunities.

JASON: Because Grandma played collegiate field hockey, didn't she?

MAMA KELCE: Yeah, she did. There were some sports that you could do that with, but not in the ones that I was interested in, like basketball and baseball. But I did softball when I got into the corporate arena. And also darts.

JASON: Darts?!

MAMA KELCE: I don't know if you could consider that a sport, but I was on a team. We were in the all-girls league and I did that a lot before you guys.

TRAVIS: This is great.

JASON: Time-out, how did we not know this?

MAMA KELCE: I don't know, you've never asked.

JASON: I love darts!

TRAVIS: I got a dartboard right here. I got it right over there.

MAMA KELCE: I don't know if I could do it. That's something you have to do a lot of.

TRAVIS: Oh, stop it. Mom!

MAMA KELCE: Constantly, in order to be good.

JASON: It's like riding a bike. It's going to be a little rusty to start off, but you'll be right there.

TRAVIS: You're talking to two of your offspring. We have the same genes as you. You can just pick that thing up and throw bull's-eye.

MAMA KELCE: I had to practice for a little while, but yeah, I did darts and whatever I could get involved in. I did a little bit of soccer, but I'm not an endurance runner. I'm a sprinter.

JASON: Same.

TRAVIS: Yeah, same.

MAMA KELCE: Couldn't do the soccer thing. I enjoyed it.

TRAVIS: Who were your teams growing up? Was it all Cleveland-based or were you biased a little bit to some other teams?

MAMA KELCE: No, I stayed true to the Cleveland Browns and the Cavs.

TRAVIS: Thatta way, Mom. True Clevelander right there.

MAMA KELCE: Yeah, I stay with the Cleveland teams.

TRAVIS: Have you seen the Browns' new quarterback?

MAMA KELCE: Yes, I have.

TRAVIS: Have you seen some highlights from him? He's doing pretty good.

MAMA KELCE: Yeah, he is. They're doing very well. They're getting hot right now.

JASON: Smoking Joe.

TRAVIS: Smoking Joe, Joe Flacco. Sounds about right. That was, Mom is definitely one of the people who brought sports into our lives. So yes, she's always been a sports fan.

MAMA KELCE: I can honestly say that your dad was the one that searched out teams and things like that. And we just shared getting you to wherever you needed to go and whatever sport you wanted to play. So we followed you. Whatever sport you wanted to play, that's what we did.

JASON: How did we get into sports? Did we just go into things that our friends did? It's hard to remember back to like when we first started.

MAMA KELCE: As early as we could, when you were about three, you were playing soccer in North Ridgeville.

JASON: Wow.

TRAVIS: How rough was that to watch?

MAMA KELCE: It was like a herd. Kids would just move around the field in a herd. Everybody was around the ball. It was funny. That's kind of the way hockey was, too, when you were six.

TRAVIS: Just watching some of those home videos you took of us outside and Dad not being able to keep the camera on the puck.

MAMA KELCE: It's hard to do!

TRAVIS: It was tough to watch.

MAMA KELCE: Yeah. But it was fun getting you involved in hockey. That's when we finally moved to Cleveland Heights and they had a rink, and it wasn't as far away to drive. So those were great times. We had family friends that were involved in hockey, and they got us into it. It was really the Halls.

JASON: The Halls, and there was a lot of community involvement in hockey, which kind of caused us to start doing it. Lacrosse, the same way. Terry Saylor was the coach of the girls' team at the high school.

TRAVIS: Shout-out to Mr. Saylor.

JASON: And he was always trying to push us into lacrosse, and we tried it one year and got into that.

MAMA KELCE: And that was because it was a crossover from hockey into lacrosse.

JASON: Yeah, the sports didn't conflict, and you could hit people.

MAMA KELCE: Yeah, the only thing that a boy likes better than running downfield with a stick is running downfield with a stick and two knives on their feet.

TRAVIS: Jesus, Mom.

MAMA KELCE: Well, that's what skates are. They're blades.

TRAVIS: You're right. Unfortunately, yeah.

MAMA KELCE: What more could you want? It's sad, but true. But anyway, it was fun.

TRAVIS: It still is. Let's get to Donna Bold Holiday Topics. About to force everybody into Kelce Christmas here. What was your favorite gift that you got this year?

MAMA KELCE: Oh, man, that's tough.

TRAVIS: You have to choose.

JASON: That means she didn't get anything good. Just for anybody watching. "Favorite gift, huh? Don't really have one."

TRAVIS: Just wait until she comes to Kansas City.

JASON: There you go.

TRAVIS: I got you covered. I got the family covered.

MAMA KELCE: You know, really, Christmas is about giving. It's not about receiving. But I did get some really nice earrings. I have to admit.

TRAVIS: Niiiiice!

JASON: You still have one of your gifts.

TRAVIS: Jason's still getting you earrings, huh?

JASON: Yeah.

MAMA KELCE: Hey, I do like earrings. For some reason, you think I don't like them. The sweatshirt and the mug with your pictures on it were great the first couple of times, but every year it kind of got old. But I do love jewelry, so that was always a plus.

TRAVIS: What was the kind of earring that we always got you, though? It was the certain type of rock or something?

MAMA KELCE: It was hoops. And those are always good. You can wear those anytime.

What is a favorite piece of football/sports memorabilia that you guys own?

92%er: ksd_13 via Club 92

TRAVIS: I can't tell you exactly what I own, but I got some good shit and I'm very proud of it. One of the coolest items that I have is right here on my desk since Jason got it for me.

JASON: Don't say that one. Don't say that one.

TRAVIS: It's a Babe Ruth, Baby Ruth, grade nine, which is out of ten. It's a pretty goddamn good grade. It's got a Babe Ruth signature baseball right here from back in the day. And it looks like it's got a few other people on it, too . . . who's Henry Williams? This is pretty fucking good. Who's that on the bottom? Bob Feller. Who's Bob Feller?

JASON: Legendary Cleveland Indian baby.

TRAVIS: This is the coolest thing that I've ever gotten from Jason for sure. I might go play catch with it or something. Play a little sandlot baseball with it.

JASON: Play a little pickup baseball with the dog. What is it about a baseball? A signed baseball is the best.

TRAVIS: It's our childhood, man.

JASON: I don't know why. It's just like ingrained in my head.

TRAVIS: Did you ever get anybody to sign a baseball when you were younger? Like the satisfaction of it?

JASON: I went and waited in the Cleveland Indians parking lot.

TRAVIS: We did that after every fucking game. Dad took me down there.

JASON: I remember when you got to go down with Dad. We had two tickets. You guys had fun. That was great.

TRAVIS: You went the year before.

JASON: Not to the All-Star Game. There isn't an All-Star Game every year in Cleveland, Travis.

TRAVIS: You didn't even like baseball, though. Dad knew I would fuckin' appreciate it more and I would remember it more. And I did.

JASON: My favorite piece of sports memorabilia is actually very timely because this person just passed away Monday night while I was doing Monday night countdown, which made it hit extra hard. Well, at least that's when the news broke. Pete Rose. I have a signed baseball by Pete Rose.

TRAVIS: Charlie Hustle himself, man.

JASON: I've always been a huge Pete fan. Obviously, he had his demons, but the way he played the game and carried himself. And I think also Dad just loved him, so that made me love him a little bit more. So I love that piece of memorabilia that will probably mean more now that there won't be any more of 'em made.

TRAVIS: I've had a lot of people run into Pete before he passed, and they said great things about him. Either way, RIP to the big guy, and that is a very, very cool piece of memorabilia that you got. What else do you got? You got anything else?

JASON: I also have some boxes of football cards that are from Tom Brady's rookie year—I brought this up on an earlier show—that I really want to open. I still haven't opened them, but I think it would be cool to open those. Maybe that can be bonus content. I don't know. I think it would be fun. Open them and see if there's a Tom Brady rookie card inside.

TRAVIS: Dude, I'd be at the edge of my seat watching that fucking thing if you're opening those.

JASON: Can you imagine we open one of them, we pull a freaking Tom Brady rookie card?

TRAVIS: I want to know who else is in that draft class.

JASON: I know that Tom's the big-ticket item. Let's look. He's the big ticket because that's the one that's going for millions of dollars signed and like delivered. What was Tom's rookie year?

TRAVIS: '01.

JASON: Two thousand draft? Courtney Brown, Cleveland Brown. Hale, 2000 NFL Draft. LaVar Arrington, Peter Warrick, Jamal Lewis, Corey Simmons, Corey Simon? Corey Simmons? I should know him from the Philadelphia Eagles.

TRAVIS: I feel like there's a better way to go about this.

JASON: Brian Urlacher. It's huge, Urlacher. I'll go crazy if I get an Urlacher card 'cause I love Brian Urlacher.

JASON: Yeah. I'm really hoping for that Tom Brady after looking at some of these names.

NEW DUMB QUESTION

What sucked as a child, but is lit as an adult?

**92%er: krispwah_destination
via Reddit**

TRAVIS: Beer! Beer sucked as a kid. I stole a sip from my dad's beer, it was fucking disgusting.

JASON: How old were you when you did that? I feel like I did it, too, when I was young and Dad swears up and down he didn't let that happen. But I'm pretty sure I did try it and it was disgusting.

TRAVIS: It was dog shit.

JASON: Playing baseball. There's nothing worse than sitting in the outfield and just praying that your pitcher gets shelled so you can actually do something.

Naps. Great. That's a great one.

TRAVIS: Naps didn't suck as a child for me. I fucking love naps.

JASON: I didn't like going to bed when I was younger. I wanted to stay up and now I can't wait to be able to go to bed. It's the highlight of my day.

TRAVIS: I still love naps.

JASON: Poetry? Coffee?

TRAVIS: Coffee's another one—coffee, beer. Not that I was drinking coffee or beer, I had a sip of it and it was like, what the fuck are you guys drinking that for? And then never drank it again until I was an adult.

JASON: Reading? Reading's weird because my kids are so young, they love reading kids' books, but I feel like there's a time period when I was younger where I just didn't really like reading. And now when I have the time, I fucking love reading a book. I do mostly Audible because I don't have the time to physically read books. But whenever I take the time to do it, I'm very happy that I read a book.

TRAVIS: I'm still out on reading.

2

Relationships, Marriage, and Parenting

My girlfriend and I have talked about getting married and she wants a fall wedding and I told her, good luck with that because I'm going to be at a football game. What's your opinion on fall weddings?

92%er: William from Montgomery via the Heights Hotline

JASON: Sounds like this marriage is going to work out great.

TRAVIS: I actually don't know people who have gotten married in the fall because all the weddings I've been to and all my friends always do it in the summer.

JASON: Yeah, we can't go usually.

TRAVIS: Jason's pretty spot-on, you guys got to be more in sync on things. You got to be willing to find a weekend where the team isn't playing anybody good maybe. Also, if you really do have a problem with that, maybe it's in her best interest to not have it in the fall so that she knows you're invested in the anniversary every time it comes around.

You guys should duke that out. I don't think we have any say on what you should be doing here. And I've seen weddings in fucking February. I've seen weddings every time but the fall. So I'm not sure if the fall is a good wedding season.

JASON: Brother, I'm going to tell you right now, do the fall and the wedding and avoid this frivolous fight that means absolutely fucking nothing. You can watch the football game. Like . . . record it and watch it again. I don't know what you want me to say. There are certain things that are more important than football. And if the wedding isn't more important than football, we got some bigger issues here. I get what you're saying. You can do it another time. Just speaking from experience. There's a lot of days in the fall that there's not football. We can't find a—

TRAVIS: Like name one.

JASON

THERE ARE CERTAIN THINGS THAT ARE MORE IMPORTANT THAN FOOTBALL.

JASON: Well, depending on whether he goes to college and NFL games on Sunday, like you can go on a Friday. You can have a wedding on a Friday.

TRAVIS: Yeah, but it's a weekend thing. It's a whole weekend thing. Don't make my friends have to not go. Everybody's got season tickets, all right? Don't make my friends have to choose whether or not they have to sell their tickets that week.

JASON: There's a lot more important things than football. And weddings happen to be one of them. And "not arguing with your wife" is high up there with "more important than football." So I would just do the wedding whenever she wants to, because that's kind of your job now.

TRAVIS: "Football is life, football is life."

What would you do if you lived in a split household who root for rival schools?

92%er: Jordan from Chicago via the Heights Hotline

JASON: Listen, I kind of like that. I always enjoy ribbing my buddies and friends.

TRAVIS: That's the best, that's the best part of being fans.

JASON: If you have a healthy fandom, you enjoy the back-and-forth with the rivals, right?

TRAVIS: Yeah, hell yeah.

JASON: Talking trash, the different bets. I think there's something exciting about that. I also want to know what the specific teams are. Is it Ohio State–Michigan?

TRAVIS: Yeah, maybe.

JASON: Like Auburn-Alabama? I don't know.

TRAVIS: I don't know either. But what are some fun bets? Who's got to take out the trash, who's got to do the dishes, who's got to change the diapers, who's got to, you know . . .

JASON: Putting chores on the line is always a good one.

TRAVIS: Wearing the other person's team into work or something, make you feel real stupid out in public.

JASON
PUBLIC HUMILIATION IS ALWAYS A GOOD THING

JASON: That is good. Public humiliation is always a good thing to put on the line. You could definitely go with, you know, throw a little bit of that like, "Hey. Loser's gotta do a favor."

TRAVIS: Not again.

JASON: I'm already in a . . . Kylie took to Twitter [X] announcing that I'm already in a—

TRAVIS: The doghouse.

JASON: Not the doghouse. I'm in a dry spell right now, so I don't wanna get into any more trouble with Ky.

TRAVIS: This is what being a diehard fan is about, though. Having the fun back-and-forth, even if it's with a loved one. I mean even more so, right? It's so much fun because you know the person's true intentions, you're not gonna get insulted by what they're saying, so really lay it on them. Make them feel real stupid for being a part of that fan base.

JASON: Yeah. In a playful way. In a playful way.

TRAVIS: Yeah, of course. Always in a playful way. Never take it too serious, no.

What's up, fellas? I'm a Lions fan, but I love the show. I'm 18, so I'm not a parent. But I was going to ask, what advice would you give to a parent that wants to teach their kid how to be better at golf? I'm just . . . I'm really, I'm really bad at golf, guys. And I, you know, I need help. So. Help me, please.

92%er: Noah via the Heights Hotline

JASON: Did you say I'm eighteen, so I'm not a parent? What the fuck does that mean? Such a weird way to ask us to help him with his golf game. "Hey, I'm Noah. I'm eighteen. So I'm not a parent." And I was like, what the fuck, where are we going with this?

TRAVIS: He just wants to let everybody know he's the child in this. He wants advice to tell his parents on what to do to make him a better golfer, it sounds like.

JASON: From two football players.

TRAVIS: I consider myself an average golfer. I would say first thing is probably the thing that you've already considered. And that's get lessons.

JASON: Nah.

TRAVIS: Nah, you're right. The rule of ten thousand, bud, just pick up a stick and go hit that fucking thing, man.

JASON: My number one thing is just play a bunch of golf.

TRAVIS: Dude, just go out there. Every lie is going to be different. You're going to need to have a few extra balls in your pocket when you go and play golf the next time, not so you can cheat, so you can take the same shot multiple times. That way you're getting used to taking all the different random-ass, above-your-feet, below-your-feet, behind, up a hill, down at like the slopes and all the divots and all the different types of grass.

There's so many different fucking shots. You're going to be overwhelmed by it if you just jump into it. But it's going to be fun. I got a good friend right now that's actually picking up the sticks for the first time, man. And he was fucking *hacking* it. He was *hacking* it out.

JASON: Get the fuck out of here.

TRAVIS: It was funny to see him get into it. Every single shot, after every single hole he's like, "You just have so much more respect for the pros." And I'm like, "Bro, you are so far behind what the pros are, where they started and all this. Dude, don't even think that you were going to come out here and hit a shot like a pro. Like you got your swing." The biggest thing is, you get out there. You just fucking hack. You figure out things and get on the Instagram. Just start scrolling the reels, typing golf at the top, hear how people talk about golf. If you really want to get good at it, just engulf yourself in the knowledge.

JASON: *[laughing]* Engulf yourself.

TRAVIS: Yeah, there you go.

JASON: That's great. All right.

TRAVIS: Engulf yourself, engulf everything.

JASON: Yeah, this is all good advice. The biggest thing is practice, right? If you take anything you do, anything you want to get better at, you just practice at it. But not just practice. You put practice in with a purpose, right?

TRAVIS: Oh, the P&P.

JASON: Take this from me. Listen, I am the third-to-last-place finisher of the American Century Classic last year. So take my advice. Practice with the clubs you're going to use the most. So what club you're going to use the most on a golf course? Driver, putter. Putter more. If you two-putt every hole, you're going to beat most people you play with. Next club? Driver, right? Then your wedges. Get really good at those three things. And you're going to be a decent golfer. You're going to shoot a pretty good score. So go to a chipping green, get really good at chipping, up and downs, and then always two-puttin'. Dude, you're going to be golden, bubba. You're going to be sitting pretty.

TRAVIS: I haven't played golf with you in forever. I can't wait.

3

Holidays

What's your favorite Fourth of July memory?

92%er: @holdontoswift via X

JASON: I don't know, drinking beer and eating hot dogs.

TRAVIS: Lighting fireworks.

JASON: We never did. We could talk about this. We were not a fireworks household.

TRAVIS: Oh, I'm a fireworks man now. I fucking love fireworks, dude.

JASON: Growing up.

TRAVIS: No, Ed was not a—

JASON: No, that was a hard no.

TRAVIS: It was a hell no. I think Dad and Aunt Judy knew someone at a young age that blew off their hand or something like that.

JASON: That'll turn you off of fireworks.

TRAVIS: Especially kids around fireworks. Obviously, the sparklers are cool, but even the little smoke bombs are a little too much.

JASON: I'm not going to lie. I do not like lighting any of those things anywhere in my vicinity. I am out on the fireworks. Love watching them. Like our neighbor has a great fireworks display. I'm going to their house for sure to watch the fireworks, but I am not going anywhere near the mother-fuckers.

TRAVIS: Nice. I hear you.

JASON: I'm terrified of them.

TRAVIS: I will say this. I am a huge fan of them. If you're looking for fireworks in the States—

JASON: I know exactly where you're going.

TRAVIS: Shameless plug here. One of my favorite families in the world, the Zoldans. They have a fireworks company. Everybody, go make sure you hit up Phantom Fireworks. They're all over the States. They're the number one firework distributor *in the country*, I would say. I'm going to say in the world just because I love them the most. But a great family and they got great stuff if you walk in there. So shout-out to the Zoldans and shout-out to Phantom Fireworks.

But moving on to my favorite Fourth of July memory. I can't really say. I will say, and we were talking about this earlier about the story that you might tell here, but it's going down to Lake Lanier with the Halls and the Air Force guys.

JASON: Chad, Kelly, now Stafford, all the Air Force guys. Yeah, that was special.

TRAVIS: That was something I remember forever for sure.

JASON: There is something around being around servicemen around Fourth of July that just makes it like that much more meaningful. It really hits you more, I feel like. It's hard to come up with a great memory of Fourth of July because it's really just being around the people. It always comes down to family, friends. It's the one day that we all get to celebrate that we're in this country together. Thanksgiving is more family oriented. Fourth of July is like, "We're America, bubba, and this is the big day that we became America. So we're going to celebrate the one thing that we all have in common, which is that we are Americans."

And the memories that you share are the ones that come down to you being with your fellow Americans and celebrating that we're all from the same country and that we get the freedoms to enjoy all of these wonderful [things]. And it's a special day to think back to the people that have fought, including the people especially in the Revolutionary War that led to July 4th. But all of the men and women that have fought for this country. All of the men and women that—

TRAVIS: Protect this country today, yeah.

JASON: Not just protect it, but this country has become what it is because of all of its fine inhabitants that make it special. It's a day to really think about that. And is it perfect? No, nobody's perfect. I would say *a lot* of really, you know, terrible things in its past. But God damn, I'm really happy of the people that are in this country, of the friends and family members and ones that I get to share this nation with. So it's just a wonderful day. And that's what it comes down to. As well as barbecue and beer and water if you're around it maybe.

TRAVIS: Couldn't have said it any better, brother.

JASON: So to everybody looking to have fun on the Fourth of July, have fun—

TRAVIS: Be safe.

JASON: But be smart. There's stuff . . . there's so much stupid shit that happens every year with fireworks, with water. Just be smart. Have fun. Enjoy being an American with fellow Americans or with other people, whoever wants to celebrate it. Be a smart person.

What was your favorite Halloween costume and who got the most candy?

92%er: @lisadavis4459 via YouTube

JASON: The only one I really remember is when we went as Mario and Luigi in Cleveland Heights High School.

TRAVIS: Who's got that fucking picture, man? You see how ecstatic I was to be Luigi, man.

JASON: You'll see what it feels like to be a younger brother and your older brother forces you into doing something.

TRAVIS: Comes home with some overalls and then—what are they—Mickey Mouse hands?

JASON: I don't know what it was. But it worked. It was a good outfit.

TRAVIS: It was definitely funny and like for whatever reason, you definitely look like Mario and I look like a long, thin Luigi. It was pretty good.

JASON: I will say Halloween somewhat got ruined for us by Dad because we stopped at a very young age.

TRAVIS: He's the Grinch of Halloween. He'll still pass out candy.

JASON: He just doesn't want to walk up and down the street with you. Maybe that was the real reason. But the way he said it to us was "Once you stop trick-or-treating, you've hit another level of maturity." He hated if anybody was even remotely at puberty level; if you were trick-or-treating, you were not getting candy at the Kelce household. He would actively reject people. He would say, "No."

TRAVIS: "Beat it."

JASON: "Get out of here. Not young enough." So we stopped before we got to middle school.

TRAVIS: It was definitely before middle school.

JASON: We were young and it was kind of fun. Then we got to scare kids and we'd hide in leaf piles.

TRAVIS: TPing people's houses and egging people's cars. Of course . . . kids, don't do that to people, all right?

JASON: No, definitely do that to people. That's Halloween.

TRAVIS: No, the egging cars was too much for me.

JASON: Do all that. Screw that. Get into trouble, kids.

TRAVIS: Do all that? I'm going to walk outside and my house is going to be TPed and all my cars are going to be egged.

JASON: Don't do it to my house, but definitely go out there and do it because you're kids. That's what you're supposed to do. Go get into some trouble. Within reason!

TRAVIS: "Within reason!" Ed Kelce's number one rule. You could be stupid. Just don't be real stupid. That's actually a Stevie Bogas rule, man. Shout-out to Stevie Bogas.

JASON: Shout-out to Stevie.

TRAVIS: Stevie, we love you, big guy.

JASON: We miss you. We love ya, Stevie.

Yeah, Halloween candy. While we did trick or treat, what was our favorite Halloween candy? I can tell you it definitely wasn't candy corn. We've already been through that. One of the most overrated corns or candy is candy corn.

TRAVIS: Who doesn't love frosting? That's all it is, just pure sugar. There's no way you hate it.

JASON: First of all, I don't like frosting that much.

TRAVIS: You don't like frosting?!

JASON: It has to be the right amount. I will actively take frosting off a cake.

TRAVIS: *[holding his thumb and index finger about an inch apart]* It's got to be like this much, right? Like this much frosting?

JASON: I don't know. It depends on how thick the cake is. Listen, if candy corn was melted and put on cake, it might taste okay, but it's not. It's solid and chalky, and it has no business being eaten on a holiday or being represented as the gold standard of a holiday.

TRAVIS: It's festive, Jason.

JASON: Listen, would you rather have candy corn or Reese's, okay?

TRAVIS: I'm not putting it over Reese's. Reese's Pieces at that.

JASON: Well, that's what we're talking about. Let's stop talking about candy corn. What are the best Halloween candies? What were you always excited about when you got in your bag? Starburst, always excited about Starburst, always excited.

TRAVIS: I was a Milky Way kid.

JASON: Anything chocolate. Snickers, Twix—

TRAVIS: *Twix!*

JASON: Kit Kat. I'm a big Kit Kat guy, love Kit Kat.

TRAVIS: Kit Kat's got a little overrated until they made the white chocolate ones, and that switched it up, got me back on the Kit Kat train.

JASON: I like Kit Kat original more than white chocolate. Ooh, Nerds.

TRAVIS: Nerds are always bangers.

JASON: Those are so good.

TRAVIS: God damn, I could go for some Nerds right now.

JASON: Cleveland Heights had like a lot of former hippies, and some people that were very health-conscious.

TRAVIS: Former? Still *thriving* hippies, are you kidding me?

JASON: That's a good point. I guess once a hippie, always a hippie.

TRAVIS: You don't get off that train. You're on that thing for life.

JASON: Either way, Cleveland Heights had some houses that would give you an apple. Do you remember that?

TRAVIS: Fuck no.

JASON: I remember just being furious. I wasn't putting an apple in my frigging trick-or-treat bag. There's no way. As soon as I got that apple, I was walking away and throwing it at the house.

TRAVIS: At the house?

JASON: So hopefully it exploded.

TRAVIS: "Get some candy!"

JASON: Unacceptable. Is there a bigger, like, litmus test for whether you're a good person than the people that aren't home, so they just leave a big tub of candy out front with the sign that says only take one?

TRAVIS: Oh, that's getting fucking raided. I did that not too long ago.

JASON: Dude, I never. I always just took one.

TRAVIS: You're a good kid. Unsupervised? I'm taking the whole fucking thing. Are you kidding me?

JASON: What about all the kids after you, Travis?

TRAVIS: Snooze you lose, man. You got to be quicker. There's candy all over the place. There's no shortage of candy around here. If you let me put my hand in your candy bag in your house, I wasn't just taking one. I was fucking— *[mimics grabbing with whole hand]* —how much candy can I get?

JASON: Please take *one*! So this is where you would look at it from a legal standpoint when it said, "Please take one." You automatically instead of "one piece of candy" it's like "one handful."

TRAVIS: In my mind, I'm like, yo, that was always the ultimate goal was to see how much candy I could get.

JASON: That's the game of Halloween.

TRAVIS: If you're not supervising me, I'm just going to—

JASON: But that's cheating. That's like taking steroids. You gotta abide by the rules.

TRAVIS: Nah, nah, nah, nah, nah, nah. That's just flanking. That's all this is. Catch them while they're not at the front porch.

JASON: Do you guys get trick or treaters? Unfortunately, we don't get trick or treaters.

TRAVIS: A hundred percent, dude. My street right now is absolutely lit every single year.

JASON: Love it.

TRAVIS: So much fun.

JASON: Do you give out? What do you do? Give out real-size candy bars?

TRAVIS: I did . . . I got got.

JASON: What do you mean, you got got?

TRAVIS: I didn't know if everybody knew where I lived at the moment. And of course, everyone knows at this point. It's all good, though. I love Kansas City. Just being there handing out candy would have probably been a little aggressive. I just put it out on the front porch. I didn't say, "Please take one." I put a bunch of like big king-size candy bars in there. And I was like, "All right, I'll just see if everybody gets it." And sure enough, like the first group of fucking twelve-year-olds come by and just— *[mimics grabbing the whole bag]* —basically just ran with the entire bag.

JASON: You know how this works, Travis.

TRAVIS: Yeah, you're right. I thought, "I grew up on the east side of Cleveland.

It's a little different over there. I'm over here in North KC. It's a nice neighborhood." I didn't know.

JASON: Nah, kids are kids.

TRAVIS: I don't know if kids are supervised doing this or not, you know. Who knows? But I definitely got got doing what I did to other households as a kid, so—

JASON: Hey, comes full circle.

TRAVIS: Karma's real. You got to love it, man. Wasn't even upset. I just screamed at them as they were running away, "Get back here!"

JASON: Next no dumb question.

TRAVIS: No, no, no, no. Hold on. You got to answer this. Are you handing out candy?

JASON: We don't have sidewalks, so we don't have trick or treaters, unfortunately.

TRAVIS: What a fucking . . . so where do you do it? You're taking the girls over by Dad's?

JASON: Either that or Kylie's taking the girls over to her parents' house.

TRAVIS: Nice.

JASON: And then they walk around the streets there. And I think her parents both give out regular-size candy bars.

TRAVIS: King-size? Regular?

JASON: I don't know if it's king-size, but it's not the fun size. It's like a standard.

TRAVIS: If you're going to go king-size, you got to buy so much because it's like your ammo. You just don't have as much ammo.

JASON: I don't think kids should get king-size. I think a regular candy bar is about as high as you should probably go. Or if you really care, you give them an apple apparently.

Since Thanksgiving is around the corner, what is your favorite dish and what is one that you absolutely hate?

92%er: YRod13 via Club 92

JASON: Let's take it one step further and rank the top five classic Thanksgiving sides. And let's also throw in some ones that we absolutely can't stand, which I feel like there's a bunch. Travis is super picky. Our Thanksgiving—we've talked about this before. It always ended in tears.

TRAVIS: Don't take me back.

JASON: With Travis at the table, Dad screaming at him.

TRAVIS: Don't take me back. *[pretending to cry]* I'm thankful.

JASON: *[mimicking their dad yelling]* "Eat the food! Be thankful!"

All right, here we go. My must-haves. Mama Kelce dinner rolls.

TRAVIS: Gotta have.

JASON: Do yourself a favor, get some Mama Kelce dinner rolls. Gosh, I'm going green bean casserole.

TRAVIS: Okay.

JASON: Mashed potatoes.

TRAVIS: Okay.

JASON: Corn, not candy corn, *corn*. And then there has to be some type of meat. I know everybody says turkey. I think turkey has to kind of be there. But if I'm not lying, we were always a big pork chop family growing up. And pork chops taste better than turkey, if I'm being honest, so . . .

TRAVIS: Yeah, I'm going ham. I'm going honey baked ham.

JASON: Honey baked ham. God damn it. We had that too. Fuck.

TRAVIS: Honey baked ham with the pineapple.

JASON: I should have chose that. Can I change? It's too late to change?

TRAVIS: Too late.

JASON: Can I change?

TRAVIS: You already said fucking whatever you just said.

JASON: Pork chop?

TRAVIS: Yeah.

JASON: All right. You got me there. Honey baked ham for sure.

TRAVIS: The pork chops were solid though.

JASON: They were. Yeah. Mom did a good job with those.

TRAVIS: I'm going ham first. You got to have honey baked ham, that sugar crust. Maybe throw some pineapples in there.

JASON: That was a huge miss by me. Good job. You nailed it.

TRAVIS: It's the best. What else? Mac and cheese. Got to have some mac and cheese.

JASON: Yeah, I mean, it's—

TRAVIS: *Got to* have mac and cheese.

JASON: I respect it. I respect it.

TRAVIS: That's where this gets tricky for me.

JASON: Those are like the only three that are really that important.

TRAVIS: Everything else is just like whatever.

JASON: Whatever else you want to put on the table, as long as those three are there.

TRAVIS: Get some of Mama Kelce's dinner rolls. Get some Hawaiian rolls in there.

JASON: Well, that's almost like a necessity with the honey baked ham.

TRAVIS: One hundred percent.

JASON: I guess probably our biggest Thanksgiving staple that we absolutely hated growing up, I think we have to both absolutely say turkey.

TRAVIS: I'm out on stuffing.

JASON: Oh, I like stuffing.

TRAVIS: I'm out on casseroles really.

JASON: I'm not with you on any of this.

TRAVIS: You know what I do like is yams, candied yams. Candied yams, those are fucking, I mean . . .

JASON: We never had the cranberry sauce with the turkey. For some reason, we didn't do that when we did do it. It's a game changer. I mean, you basically just coat it in sugar. Shocker, it ends up being delicious.

TRAVIS: I'm out on cranberry sauce.

JASON: The other big thing is that we always put it in the oven. I gotta deep-fry one this year. Have you ever deep-fried one?

TRAVIS: Look at me. No.

JASON: Okay. I don't know what "look at me" means.

TRAVIS: I've never cooked a turkey ever in my life.

THE OTHER BIG THING IS THAT WE ALWAYS PUT IT [THE TURKEY] IN THE OVEN. I GOTTA DEEP-FRY ONE THIS YEAR. HAVE YOU EVER DEEP-FRIED ONE?

TRAVIS

LOOK AT ME. NO.

JASON: I smoked one, one year. It was really good too. A little spatchcock. The first deep-fried turkey we ever had was over at the Woodworths' house when we went over there for Thanksgiving. I remember how incredibly juicy and delicious it was. So, I think I'm going to try and deep-fry it and not burn my house down. But it's just . . . everything tastes better deep-fried, right?

TRAVIS: Yeah, can't go wrong with that one. That's all I got for you, man. Ham, mac and cheese, and rolls, that's all I got.

JASON: I think pumpkin pie is pretty overrated.

TRAVIS: You're going to get cracked for that.

JASON: I'm going to get crushed for it, but I would much rather have pecan pie.

TRAVIS: I'm not big on pie anyways. I'm not a pie guy.

JASON: I'm with you there. Apple pie, I'm not going to lie. So average. The most overrated dessert in the history. The only reason I like apple pie is because usually people put a scoop of ice cream with it.

TRAVIS: Ooh.

JASON: Outside of that, I want nothing to do with the apple pie. It doesn't do anything. Pecan pie, though, I'll get down with some pecan pie.

TRAVIS: You're not an apple guy though. Like you don't like apple juice or eat apples.

JASON: I *looove* eating apples standard. A little honeycrisp. I like eating apples. I don't like apple juice. Applesauce can be pretty good too. That's one of the good things about having kids, you get reintroduced to applesauce. Haven't had applesauce in a minute.

TRAVIS: I'm not fucking touching applesauce, dude.

JASON: You'll find out.

Do you have the Christmas tree up before Thanksgiving?

92%er: @sophismophis via X

TRAVIS: And I'm going to say, no, you don't.

JASON: I don't think we ever had it up when we were growing up before Thanksgiving.

TRAVIS: I remember it, we always did it either the day after Thanksgiving or Thanksgiving after dinner.

JASON: I think it's nice to have the Christmas tree up for Thanksgiving. Just gonna put that out there.

TRAVIS: Two completely different holidays.

JASON: They are completely different. But with having everybody there, it's a nice visual to have the Christmas tree, I think.

TRAVIS: No, because then it feels like Christmas dinner.

JASON: But Thanksgiving is like the first time that you're kicking off for Christmas after that dinner.

TRAVIS: No, it's not. No, it's not.

JASON: I'm just saying. That's the way I feel.

TRAVIS: You're trying to mesh the two. Like it's a kickoff party to an event.

JASON: It is. That's why the next day is Black Friday. It's the number one shopped holiday for Christmas.

TRAVIS: No, no way. No way.

JASON: That's why it is. It's right after Thanksgiving.

TRAVIS: Black Friday is the kickoff then.

JASON: I'm saying having the Christmas tree there to symbolize that it's starting the next day. I do think Christmas music has to be either on Thanksgiving or after. Preferably after. I don't think Christmas music on Thanksgiving Day, that's a little bit off.

TRAVIS: It's the exact same thing. The Christmas tree and Christmas music are the exact same things.

JASON: The tree is just a visual thing. It's pretty. It's nice when you have all your family members there eating and the tree's in the background. I'm pro Christmas tree, which I have never been organized to get done before Thanksgiving or on Thanksgiving. So, it's never happened, but in my head . . .

TRAVIS: So, he's never actually done this, ladies and gentlemen. He's just in his head. He's not against it.

JASON: I've never thought about it, but I'm just thinking about it right now, and I'm kind of pro Christmas tree at Thanksgiving.

TRAVIS: You've never done it, so it doesn't fucking count.

JASON: Well, it might. Maybe we do it this year.

TRAVIS: No, it won't happen.

JASON: It might be nice.

TRAVIS: No, I don't believe you're going to do it. Well, you heard our dumb asses talking about that subject.

JASON: Yeah, I guess that's our opinion on that.

NEW DUMB QUESTION

What's the adult equivalent of finding out Santa isn't real?

JASON: Taxes. Like nothing further . . . just taxes.

TRAVIS: Yeah, I hear you on that. It's a pretty eye-opening experience.

JASON: Gets immediately taken out of the check. "I thought I was getting this . . ."

TRAVIS: Yeah, I don't even have to pay the tax. They just take it from me. I don't even have the option to be like, "Nah, I ain't paying this shit. Come and get me if you can."

JASON: Smart by the government. Very intelligent move or they probably would not get paid.

I don't know, like that Christopher Columbus was actually kind of a piece of shit?

That it's not "Berenstein" Bears. It's "Berenstain" Bears.

TRAVIS: I don't even know what you're talking about.

JASON: No? Cool. You could really input any conspiracy theory in this. If you're a conspiracy theorist.

TRAVIS: You trying to say Santa's real?

JASON: I think there was somebody a long time ago that inspired the figure of Santa. I do think that there was a person that gave gifts around the holidays in whatever culture Santa fucking originated.

TRAVIS: I don't know, maybe that adults just aren't as smart as you think they are as kids. Does that make sense?

JASON: Yeah, as a kid I thought Ed Kelce was the smartest person I'd ever met.

TRAVIS: As a kid, you look up at adults and you're like, "Oh my gosh, that guy is brilliant."

JASON: "He said things with conviction." I was like, yeah, I guess that's true.

PART 2

SPORTS

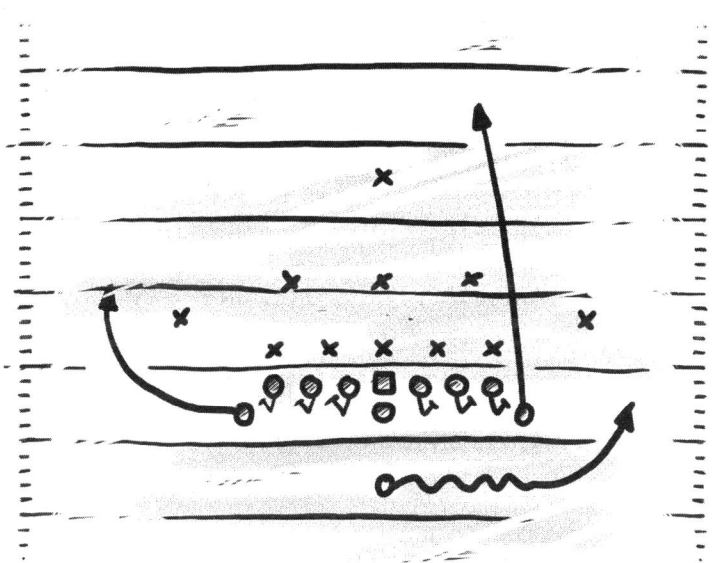

4

Football 101

What is the flag for pass interference for? Isn't the goal to interfere with the pass?

92%er: @mrob10 via YouTube

TRAVIS: I mean to an extent, yeah.

JASON: It's a fair point, mrob.

TRAVIS: You don't necessarily want to interfere. You want to more so just play the ball.

JASON: You want to interfere with the ball, not the player. I'll let Travis explain. He's a resident expert in pass interference, both offensive and defense.

TRAVIS: So pass interference is basically when a defensive player or offensive player restrict the other person from making a play on the ball. I think that's kind of the gist of it.

JASON: Yeah. When the ball is in the air, the defender can't physically impede the offensive player's ability to catch the ball. Is that a fair way?

TRAVIS: You can't impede.

JASON: So you can't go out of your way to hit the offensive player's hands or body because it would be unfair.

TRAVIS: You can go for the ball because you have a right to make a play on the ball. But if you're holding a guy and restricting him or he has to strain through contact—

JASON: —or you tackle him. These are all illegal ways to defend the pass, offensively and defensively.

TRAVIS: The ref is kind of like judging it. Some guys will let you play a little more physical. Some guys, they don't want the grabbing or anything like that.

JASON: I'm glad we're bringing this up, because a couple of years ago, they actually made defensive pass interference or offensive pass interference a reviewable play. And one of the reasons I'm against that is because when you slow things down, it appears different than what happens at real speed. And that call in particular is such a subjective call for the official. I think it's important to see what happens in real time. And there's going to be times you disagree with it, there's going to be times where you think it's a no-brainer. But I'm in big favor of leaving that on the officials. Trav, you've played a long time in the NFL at this point. Are there certain officials that you know call that differently?

TRAVIS: No, I feel like I just play the game how I feel like I can get open.

JASON: Whatever works.

Why do some touchdown celebrations get fined and others do not? What is not allowed?

92%er: Jjsodapop via Club 92

JASON: There are certain things that definitely aren't allowed. You can't use a prop. That is the big one.

TRAVIS: Except for a football. Football is the only prop you can use.

JASON: You can use the football, but you can't use the pylon. You can't touch the goalpost. Those are the big ones. You can't use pylons. You can do choreographed ones, but they can't be long, right? Do you know what that stipulation is?

TRAVIS: I don't think there's a time limit. I think you're just dealing with the play clock. As long as the guys that aren't on field goal get off the field in time for the kick. I don't think there's a time limit.

JASON: I thought there was like a time period.

TRAVIS: I could be wrong about this.

JASON: Well, you know more about touchdown celebrations than I do. Half the time I'm walking off the field because I'm trying to get my fat ass on the bench and get some oxygen.

TRAVIS: No, no, no. You're over there celebrating. Don't act like you aren't in there celebrating.

JASON: Sometimes. If it's a big play and I still got fresh legs, I'm celebrating. But if it's after a grueling drive, I am deep-breathing my ass to the sideline, high-fiving people on the way to the bench. I don't think I've ever celebrated a tush push or brotherly shove touchdown. It is like, I just scream and then yell off the field.

Do you preplan your touchdown celebrations ever?

TRAVIS: No, I think I did one or two when I was younger. A little kid will come up and say, "Do the nae nae" or "Hit the Quan" or something. I'll do that.

JASON: So you take suggestions?

TRAVIS: I did.

JASON: You don't take suggestions anymore? That might be fun.

TRAVIS: No. Why don't you take suggestions?

JASON: I don't take suggestions because I don't score touchdowns, Travis.

TRAVIS: But you've probably done more touchdown celebrations this year than I have because you celebrate with everybody.

JASON: I've done none. What are you talking about? I haven't celebrated like any of them.

TRAVIS: You got Mossed with—

JASON: I did do that one. Yeah.

TRAVIS: Then you got another one from this year.

JASON: The dancing one from last year.

TRAVIS: Yeah, the dancing one from last year, which is an iconic one that everybody will remember forever. You did something else this year. I forget what it was.

JASON: I can't remember.

TRAVIS: Ninety-two percenters call his ass out. He definitely dances more than me. I think you just got to feel it out, man. You just get in the zone and feel the electricity of the moment. You just hit it. It's like getting on the dance floor and hearing a groove. You got to feel it out sometimes. You don't always got to have something planned.

Can you explain zone coverage?

92%er: Phattycat3 via Threads

TRAVIS: What is the mysterious zone everyone keeps imagining? And why do I always think of *Top Gun*'s "Highway to the Danger Zone"? I guess it's kind of like *Top Gun*'s "Highway to the Danger Zone," right?

JASON: Zone coverage is?

TRAVIS: Yeah.

JASON: I don't know. *[singing]* "HIGHWAY to the . . ." Well, there is a danger zone and that's a specific area and that's what zone coverage is.

TRAVIS: Why don't you go ahead and explain some zone coverage, Jason?

JASON: You're throwing this at me because you want to trap me because you know that I'm not as familiar with this as you are. But you know what? I'll take the bait.

TRAVIS: Let's hear it.

JASON: So zone coverage as opposed to man coverage is what it sounds like. Man coverage, you have the offensive player in front of you. You are locked on. That's your guy.

TRAVIS: Speaking from a defensive standpoint.

JASON: And then zone coverage, you are responsible for a portion of the field or a spot. And oftentimes that is in relation to where receivers are located and can change based on formations and structure of the offense.

TRAVIS: Very well said.

JASON: There are different types of zones.

TRAVIS: Just like there's different types of man coverage.

JASON: There is middle field open. Which would be two safeties in the middle of the field that are splitting the halves of the field or quarters.

TRAVIS: Or quarters. Nice.

JASON: Then you have middle field closed, which would be a single high safety playing the zone in the middle, deep part of the field. Middle field open coverages are typically forms of two or four. And there are combo coverages, which I will admit I am less inclined to understand. And then there is your generic cover three, which is a type of middle field closed. Another type of middle field closed would be man coverage with a single high safety in the middle. Travis, I think this is where you come in and get more detailed.

TRAVIS: That's pretty damn good, man. You could play for me any day, bud. So basically, your zone covers exactly what Jason said. You have a certain area on the field or you latch on to a specific guy if he comes through your zone, it all switches. It all depends on what kind of style defense you have and the strategy that the defensive coordinator is teaching. And that switches in every single defensive room in the league. Cover three doesn't look the same in every single defense. There's certain rules that if I got into it would get extremely complicated, but . . .

Cover three is exactly what it says. There's three people deep, cover one. There's one person deep and everyone's trying to play outside leverage on a specific man and force them to the middle of the field. Cover two, typically you have two high safeties. Cover four, there's four people deep. So it's really telling you how many people are the furthest back. And that actually tells you certain rules that the underneath guys have as well. Very, very nicely done, Jason.

JASON: So there's some zones that I am unfamiliar with.

TRAVIS: Okay, let's talk about them.

JASON: So like what is cover six? I know it's some type of two and four combined, but I don't know what it is.

TRAVIS: It actually switches in every offense too. How you label defenses switches—how you schematically label a defense—or your coaches label a defense that's going to be different in every single offense. Some people say quarter-quarter-half is cover five. Some people say quarter-quarter-half is cover six. And a combo coverage like quarter-quarter-half is two cover two on one side and cover four on the other side.

And what that does is just presents certain answers for teams if they go three by one, situations like that.

JASON: Do you think it's called right away?

TRAVIS: I think it's called right away. Some people just love to run cover two or cover four to a three-by-one, even in a two-by-two and just give certain blitz looks out of it. It can get pretty complicated, but at the end of the day, they call it quarter-quarter-half because there's quarters, there's technically three safeties deep.

JASON: If you look at the middle of the field . . .

TRAVIS: Yeah, all right, nice. If you look in the middle of the field, one half of the field is playing cover four and the other half of the field is playing cover two. So it'll look like there's three safeties deep, but you're really playing a combo coverage of a middle field open style defense. Which typically presents all the underneath guys that have inside leverage, except for the corner in cover two.

JASON: Yeah, I don't know if any of this is helping you, Phattycat.

TRAVIS: I hope we answered at least something.

JASON: Yeah, I think the bottom line is a lot of the zone coverage principles allow the defense to pass players off and sit in their areas. And there are certain route combinations and concepts that are good for different coverages, for zone or man. All of these things are called, usually with certain things in mind.

And when the defense can make these zone coverages look as similar as other zone coverages—make them all look kind of the same—it presents difficulties in trying to decide where players and defenders are going to be from a leverage standpoint. Good DCs make them all look the same, in my opinion. If you can start in the same presentation and get to it, that's when you really got something tricky going on in the back end.

TRAVIS: If you can hide it, man, it becomes tough.

JASON: It's harder to do than it sounds. And if you got some players that are horses, you can get compromised trying to hide it. But it's harder when you don't know what it's going to be. That's for sure.

TRAVIS: Anything that you can do to get the offense to be a tick off, because a lot of the offense is based off timing. The quarterback's drop when he has the ball in his hands, the timing of a certain route and over-under read. And there's so many different reads for the quarterback, but it's really based off his timing, his footwork, his feet, and his progression throughout the play. All have to match up and be in sync to get the ball out on time. And if you can get an offense to tick their feet or second-guess, that's when you got something.

Please explain the red zone.

92%er: briozing via Club 92

JASON: That's all I got. I feel like red zone had to be named by a defensive coach. If it was named by an offensive coach it'd be the green zone. Baby, it's time to go.

TRAVIS: Alert, danger, danger.

TRAVIS and JASON: *[alarm noises]*

TRAVIS: Attention, all defense, attention, all defense. They're about to fucking score.

JASON: Defensive personnel, do not miss another tackle and do not allow another catch. We are in the red zone. And I repeat code red.

TRAVIS: That's pretty good.

JASON: Basically, if you're from the 20 . . . 25?

TRAVIS: Yeah, 25.

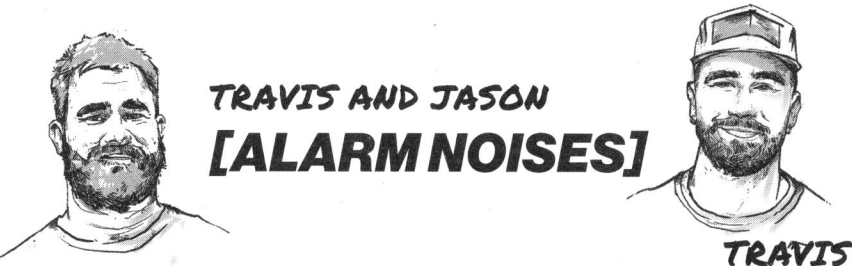

TRAVIS AND JASON
[ALARM NOISES]

TRAVIS
ATTENTION, ALL DEFENSE, ATTENTION, ALL DEFENSE. THEY'RE ABOUT TO FUCKING SCORE.

JASON: 25 is the red zone. Then there's different stipulations, even in the red zone that most offenses use.

TRAVIS: And this is where I think the terminology came from. They labeled it the red zone because a defensive coordinator would start to change his defense and modify his defense a little bit. From when you're in the middle of the field to when you're on your side of the field. So it's like they have to classify it as something, so they classify that as the red zone. What is "backed up"? The blue zone, the black?

JASON: We just call it "backed up." But I have heard it being a color zone as well.

TRAVIS: "Backed up," yeah. So to classify how teams run their style of red zone defense, they just had to group it under a word. So I think red zone has always been the consensus.

JASON: And not just red zone defense, but red zone offense. The plays you're running in that portion of the field a lot of times are much different. And then there's the red zone, which is a generic term for 25 to the goal line. But most teams even divide that up. So you have red zone, which would be like 25 to what, like the 10 or 12. Then you get into like the high red.

TRAVIS: Yeah, I don't know about all that.

JASON: Then all of a sudden, when you get to the 2 or 3, you're in the tight red.

TRAVIS: No.

JASON: No? You guys don't do any of that?

TRAVIS: I've never heard any of this. I've also been under the same classified system my entire career.

JASON: I was with Andy [Reid] and I was also with Doug [Pederson]. And I feel like we did the same thing. I think every coach I've ever had has different portions of the red zone categorized.

TRAVIS: One hundred percent, I could see that.

JASON: But maybe that's Stout [Jeff Stoutland]. All I know is from two to three yards to the goal line, that's when you have your goal line package plays. Your goal line runs are two to three yards out, usually two. But I don't even know what qualifies the high red.

TRAVIS: I don't know what the high red is yet.

JASON: And they're all differentiated. All this comes down to is offensive coordinators and defensive coordinators try to segment this, like Travis said, because the defense has changed the closer you get to the end zone.

So there's different tendencies, and the same thing with the offense. There's different tendencies that happen within different portions of that zone. So offensive coordinators and defensive coordinators differentiate when they see those tendencies shifting league-wide. Anyways, that's all I got.

TRAVIS and JASON: [alarm noises]

JASON: Alert, blitz zero, alert, blitz zero. We don't need any safeties back. Send the whole house.

TRAVIS: Blitz everyone in three, two, one . . .

What is a down? Is it like dropping the ball?

92%er: @tessaspeaknow via X

TRAVIS: No.

JASON: What is a down?

TRAVIS: A down is . . .

JASON: A down is a down.

TRAVIS: It's what we call . . .

JASON: How do you describe a down?

TRAVIS: Damn it. This is a hard-ass question. These not-dumb questions have gotten really advanced.

JASON: When an offense gets the ball, they start with first down. They have four tries to get ten yards. A down occurs when either someone has been tackled to the ground or the ball has been rendered incomplete and it moves to the next down. Unless you get ten or more yards and you get a fresh set of downs and you start over at first down. Does that sound right?

TRAVIS: I hope that sounded right because I understood everything, but I don't know . . .

TRAVIS

DAMN IT. THIS IS A HARD-ASS QUESTION. THESE NOT-DUMB QUESTIONS HAVE GOTTEN REALLY ADVANCED.

JASON: So a down is . . . you get first down, and if somebody gets tackled down, then you're on your second down attempt.

TRAVIS: You're saying so many *downs*. There's no way this is making sense.

JASON: If you throw the ball incomplete and the ball goes down, then you're on your third down chance.

TRAVIS: Every time the ball is snapped, that is a down.

JASON: A down is an attempt to get ten yards.

TRAVIS: There we go. Boom.

JASON: You get four of them to get ten yards. If you don't get ten yards in four attempts, or aka downs, then it's a turnover.

TRAVIS: Sounds good enough to me.

Tight end is a real position in American football? For serious, stop it right now.

92%er: @BeeBabs via X

TRAVIS: Yeah, tight end. You got to keep them glutes firing, man. You lose your glutes, you lose your game.

JASON: That's right. It's all about the glutes. The tight end position is basically a Chippendales position.

TRAVIS: What the fuck? A Chippendales position?

JASON: I don't know.

TRAVIS: I don't even know where you went with that. Tight end is a combo position. You do a lot of what offensive linemen do, which are the big guys like Jason. And then you do what the receivers do, which are the small, fast guys that catch the ball or receive the ball.

So basically, we're like the handyman. Whatever you need done in the house, we got you. You need some drywall, we got you. You need us to fix the faucet, we got you.

JASON: You ain't fixing no faucets.

TRAVIS: Dude, I got that.

JASON: You got the tools and everything?

TRAVIS: Just got to turn the water off first, bud.

JASON: Yeah, tight end, I think, is a reference to a receiver that is lined up tight to the end of the line.

TRAVIS: There you go.

What's a field goal?

92%er: @isaidspeaknowww via X

JASON: Dude, it's hard when something is so simple. It's hard to explain. So a field goal is when you kick the ball through the uprights.

TRAVIS: Why would you want to do that?

JASON: As an offense and you get three points. That's a field goal.

TRAVIS: You settle for three points. The goal is always to get the ball in the end zone. When you don't get the ball in the end zone and it's fourth down, typically, you settle for three points just so you can get some points on the board.

JASON: So field goal is kicking the ball from the ground through the uprights. Typically, there's a holder. You could technically do a drop kick. Not as common anymore.

No Dumb Question . . . ?

92%er: @pearlbramnick4300 via YouTube

JASON: New fan, @pearlbramnick4300. Pearl. Pearl. Dude, Pearl is a good name.

TRAVIS: Pearl is a good name.

JASON: That's an old-school . . . She's probably like seventy-five. All right, Pearl: "I learned more in like five minutes of 'No Dumb Questions' than I have from watching my husband watch football for years and having him half explain things to me as we go. Thanks, guys."

TRAVIS: This whole time, I thought we weren't making any sense at all.

JASON: Yeah, that's not a question. That's just a statement. Glad we could be of some help, Pearl.

TRAVIS: Yeah.

JASON: There were a lot of comments of like, how can people ask these questions? Listen, I'm all about expanding football's audience.

TRAVIS: This is why we're here. Come on in.

JASON: There's no dumb questions. Join the game. Whatever you think. Ask away. Have fun with it.

TRAVIS: We won't call you dumb if you ask a No-Dumb Question.

JASON: So that wasn't a question. I've read this wrong, I guess. That was just a comment. I guess Pearl's wasn't a question. I fucked that up. All right. Whatever.

Do you throw the ball or run with it?

92%er: @Themadwomanisme via X

TRAVIS: Me personally, I run with it. I've thrown it before in my day.

JASON: Well, you also catch it.

TRAVIS: I also catch it. I've thrown the ball in my day. I've thrown a touchdown before. Jason actually snaps the ball.

JASON: I throw the ball every snap, every play right between my legs.

TRAVIS: Throws it right between his legs to the quarterback.

5

In the Huddle

Why don't players squirt their own water?

92%er: @Joedfran via X

TRAVIS: That is such a good question. Somebody comes up to me with it already right here, and all they got to do is just go around from person to person, "Do you want one? I can shoot you real quick." It is convenient. I will say that.

JASON: This typically happens in like a TV time-out or something like that where you're trying to be efficient and get water to as many guys as possible before the time-out's up. So you kind of just know when somebody reaches up to squirt you to open up your mouth, and then you just get squirt. But they don't have to do the squirting. You can do the squirting sometimes, but when you develop a relationship, you just know when you're about to get squirted on and you open your mouth.

TRAVIS: You got to have a good relationship with the person squirting.

JASON: You don't want to just be letting randos squirt on you. You got to make

TRAVIS:
YOU GOT TO HAVE A GOOD RELATIONSHIP WITH THE PERSON SQUIRTING.

sure you know who you're dealing with. A trusted trainer, coach, individual, teammate. I'll let a teammate squirt me sometimes, but . . .

TRAVIS: That's just a good teammate. I'm trainer Trav, man. I got that thing right on the hip: "Need one, dude? I got you."

JASON: There's something that feels good about giving somebody a squirt. Like, it feels like you're doing them a solid. Like, I'll get you a squirt. You want some? I'll get you a squirt.

TRAVIS: Dude, have you ever trusted someone to squirt you and they just fucking miss your mouth?

JASON: Yeah, it's the worst. My pet peeve. So these Gatorade water bottles are fantastic, but sometimes they don't screw the lids on all the way. It pisses me off. Come on guys, we embarked on this avenue of trust. I opened my mouth to accept your squirt and you dumped it all down my chest. Oh man.

Is there a big group chat with the entire team for either the Chiefs and the Eagles or is there just a bunch of individual group chats?

92%er: Riley via the Heights Hotline

JASON: There's usually at least a group chat for the position group, at least for the offensive line there was.

TRAVIS: One hundred percent. We got a tight end group chat, for sure.

JASON: And usually there are more people that are active on those group chats. They're usually the more rambunctious or the people that just want to fuck around in them. But there's also like coaches in there. So I wouldn't say that those ones are the most rambunctious. I think the most rambunctious are usually the ones that are just group chats on the side with a select amount of the team or certain personalities that you just vibe with. Is that similar for you?

TRAVIS: One hundred percent. Coach Tommy Melvin, Coach Melvin, he's the one that kind of makes sure the group chat has the right guys in there. Because sometimes you got a guy kind of off and on the practice squad. You want to make sure that that guy's in the loop and informed with everything that we got coming up and the group chat is up-to-date with who's actually in the room.

Coach Melvin does it for the tight end group. But like you said, man, I have so many different football group chats from my team now, from my team back in 2016. Like the group chats, they just keep going. And it's the same with college. I still have group chats with guys from college. Me and Jason are in a few. And it's just fun, man. It's always a blast catching up and just throwing the most absurd shit in the group chat. You have to name the group chats.

JASON: Oh, what's our college group chat?

TRAVIS: We can't, Jason. No, we can't do that one.

JASON: I'm going to say it. Trailer Lite Boys.

TRAVIS: All right. Well, I'm going to politely ask that you don't put this on there, Brandon.

INTERN BRANDON: I didn't see nothing. I didn't see nothing, Travis.

I have a friend who adamantly says that head coaches that do not call plays do not matter during the actual games. We try to reason with him but he doesn't listen. Do head coaches that don't call plays matter during the games?

92%er: @ChadMasters8 via X

JASON: You want to start it off, Trav?

TRAVIS: One hundred percent. There's clock management, game management decisions that somebody has to make. Outside of the play calling, there's so much more that a head coach needs to do on game days.

Even if it's an offensive coach that does call plays, he's got to understand what's going on on the defensive side at all times. You have to know when to challenge, when not to challenge, the certain rules that are happening, especially in situational football, late in games, late in the half. There's just so much that goes into being a head coach outside of just offensive-defense play calling, that's for damn sure.

JASON: No doubt, especially as you become more aware of the different situational decisions that have to happen. I actually think it's really nice to have a coach whose sole job is to narrow in on these specific situations that only come up once a season, if that.

I kind of like it when the coach doesn't call plays. They're more involved with the team, they're more in the moment, they're more managerial, and they communicate more. I feel like calling plays is hard. You're like in it, you're trying to figure out what you're going to do the next series when you're not calling them. You know, you're busy trying to figure out what you're going to try and do next to the defense or vice versa. So I actually think a lot of the best head coaches out there don't call plays and now most of them have done it at some point. And I think it's good to have at some point called plays.

But does the head coach need to do that? I don't think he does. I actually think sometimes it winds up better just like you do, Trav. I mean, there's a good reason. Not all good play callers make good head coaches. Matter of fact, there's a lot of good play callers and good offensive or defensive minds that are not good head coaches. The bigger part of that job is, you know, being able to lead, being able to manage, being able to communicate, being able to keep everybody going in the right direction. Situational ball, all those things are more meaningful than calling plays.

We both agree with you, Chad. Your friend is really dumb.

TRAVIS: He's a dummy.

JASON: Yeah. Well, I feel like that's mean. Your friend's incorrect.

TRAVIS: Yeah. There are no dummies out here.

JASON: Do you think this is a made-up friend?

TRAVIS: Do I think this is a made-up friend?

JASON: Do you think Chad just wants to know the answer to this? So he's made up his friend, kind of like when you're trying to talk to a girl that you're a little nervous about, like, "Oh, my friend thinks you're really cute."

TRAVIS: Chad, if you're pulling one on us, man . . .

JASON: Chad, don't be afraid. Just ask the question. If that's what you want to know, just ask.

Why don't players cover their arms during bad or cold weather games? And how warm are the heated benches?

92%er: abrown32 via Club 92

TRAVIS: Benches are hot as fuck.

JASON: They're hot. They're real hot. Matter of fact, it'll burn your hamstrings sometimes if you're sitting down on it.

TRAVIS: It's got to be cold as balls for me to be on the heater, man. I don't like being overly hot or hot in general.

JASON: Yeah. If the benches are heated, I usually sit on the edge of it just so it's barely touching anything. I also don't like what it does. I feel like my cleats get softer.

TRAVIS: Yeah. I hate that.

JASON: A lot of people don't know this. There's a little floor thing that also—

TRAVIS: It's like a rubber mat that shoots up heat.

JASON: But the one thing I like heated benches for is I put my helmet down on that—

TRAVIS: Ooh, it's a good one. Makes your helmet nice and comfy.

JASON: A lot of people don't know when it gets cold out, your helmet turns into essentially—

TRAVIS: A fucking rock.

JASON: Dude, it is hard. The vet move for sure is to set that helmet right down on either the floor or you go to the jet propulsion heater on the other side and hold your helmet in front of that.

TRAVIS: Okay, jet propulsion?

JASON: Whatever that is. It looks like a jet engine. I don't know what it is.

TRAVIS: Dude, it is the jet engine heater there. I've literally seen a coat catch on fire. Dude, feathers like a fucking bird exploded. Just . . .

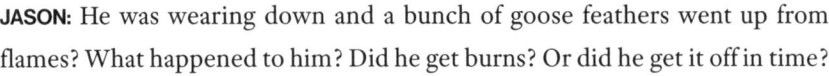

JASON: You saw it?

TRAVIS: It happened on the sideline in the game.

JASON: Oh my gosh.

TRAVIS: The jacket got caught on fire.

JASON: He was wearing down and a bunch of goose feathers went up from flames? What happened to him? Did he get burns? Or did he get it off in time?

TRAVIS: Luckily, yeah, he got it off in time.

JASON: That's crazy.

TRAVIS: Yeah, it was wild.

JASON: Was it a player or a coach?

TRAVIS: Player, player who had the long jacket on.

JASON: Gotcha. And I guess to the other question, why don't players wear sleeves, essentially, or cover their arms?

TRAVIS: It's just slicker. The new long sleeves that are like the tight-skinned long sleeves can be a little bit slicker when you put the ball away. At least that's why I don't like to wear it. I feel a lot more secure when it's just my skin on the rock. Doesn't feel as slick.

At the same time, I know a lot of guys that don't run into that problem. And a lot of the old-school, like regular cotton long-sleeve shirt or a turtleneck, a long john–type deal. The ball really doesn't slide as much on those.

JASON: Yeah, you don't want to wear that. Matter of fact, a lot of offensive coaches will not let their players wear those sleeves because they think it will affect ball security. Also when I'm cold, it's never because my arms are cold. I'm cold because my hands are cold, my feet are cold.

TRAVIS: I'm right there with you, dude. My arms and my legs don't get cold at all.

JASON: For me, if it's cold, the only thing I'm really bringing out there is one of them hand warmer pouches. In particular, because I can't wear a glove on my right hand because I snap with it, I put that sucker in there. As long as I'm moving around during the drive, I'm not really going to get cold. If I'm going to wear anything, they make these thermal-layer-like vest-type things underneath. If it's real cold, I might try that. I think I might have worn that once or twice.

TRAVIS: I know a bunch of guys are going to the scuba gear.

JASON: I tried that for warm-up. It was way too tight to me.

TRAVIS: I didn't like it. I couldn't move around. Anything that's restricting me in terms of an extra layer of clothing, I hate it. I'll just go out there regular and just be in a cut-off T-shirt and some compressions.

JASON: I want to feel nice and loosey-goosey.

Why are reporters allowed in the locker room? Do they at least give you a warning before they come in so players can cover their hairy buns and stuff?

92%er: Noel Randall via email

TRAVIS: This is a fucking fantastic question.

JASON: Hairy buns?

TRAVIS: Yeah. Well, you hit it right on the noggin. Guarantee, Jason, I haven't seen your ass in a while, but you got some hairy buns.

JASON: The carpet matches the drapes. It for sure is hairy.

TRAVIS: Yeah, we're just hairy people. Big Eddie's definitely got hairy buns. This is a good question. They do actually give us a warning. I think it's after the game's over, after meetings and everything, they give everybody like ten to fifteen minutes to kind of get situated, get dressed, or at least make yourself presentable. And then the media can just come in and it's a free-for-all.

JASON: You have like little towels.

TRAVIS: I'm not sure why. I guess it's just kind of been that way since they made this rule that, you know, the media gets like a specific, allotted time after a game instead of just making certain guys go to the podium.

JASON: Well, they can only have so many guys go to the podium. So I think the media wants this time period so they have a chance to talk to every guy, essentially, that played in the game, which doesn't always happen if you're injured or you're in a hurry. Sometimes you don't talk to the media, but for the most part, they can talk to whoever they want to in the locker room.

TRAVIS: And if you remember Marshawn Lynch: "I'm just here so I don't get fined." As a player in the NFL, you have to allocate time for the media. And if you don't, you'll get fined.

JASON: Yeah, I guess you don't have to. You can just take the fine. But if you don't want to lose money, you have to.

TRAVIS: Was it ever weird?

JASON: Is it weird having people in a locker room? I don't think it's weird.

TRAVIS: The only time I feel like it's weird is if you're like ass naked next to the guy's locker that's getting interviewed.

JASON: Yeah.

TRAVIS: Because then there's just a whole bunch of people, like media people dressed in like full-on clothes, men and women just standing next to you being ass naked. So I don't know.

JASON: I think I've just been naked in front of enough people at this point that I don't think it's really that weird.

TRAVIS: I mean, I think it was more like getting that feeling when I first got to the league. I could give a rat's ass now.

JASON: I thought it was weird in high school when guys would wear bathing suits into the showers.

TRAVIS: That was weird.

JASON: Get naked. We're all going to get naked now. It's not weird. You're making it weird by not getting naked. Now what are you trying to hide? Just be naked. You know what I mean? That's what's weird.

TRAVIS: Dude, I fully understand what you're saying.

JASON

GET NAKED. WE'RE ALL GOING TO GET NAKED NOW. IT'S NOT WEIRD. YOU'RE MAKING IT WEIRD BY NOT GETTING NAKED. NOW WHAT ARE YOU TRYING TO HIDE? JUST BE NAKED.

What contractual obligations do players have during the offseason? Like are dangerous activities off limits?

92%er: Sideboob55 via Club 92

TRAVIS: Basically, you can't get injured. If you get injured, you're fucked. So, just try and stay as safe as possible.

JASON: If you get hurt at any point in the offseason, technically that ends up being considered what they call an NFI, nonfootball injury, and you are at risk of voiding any nonguaranteed money in your contract.

There are some players that enjoy doing dangerous activities, where they will sometimes have things written into their contracts ahead of time. So, let's say they're signing a player that is a known motorcycle rider. They might write into the contract, "If you get hurt on a motorcycle, you are voiding future, even guaranteed money." That would be an addendum that a player might be signing.

There are also contractual obligations for workout bonuses. So, some guys if they don't know if they're going to show up to the facilities for offseason work-outs, they will put bonuses in there, sometimes up to $500,000 to show up and lift weights and play in the sun with a bunch of your friends. It's a pretty good deal.

TRAVIS: But other than that, it's pretty self-explanatory. If you could die doing it, like jumping out a plane, it's probably going to be frowned upon by the NFL.

JASON: But it doesn't even have to do with that. This is where it gets weird with NFI. If you're lifting weights outside the facility, like you could be trying to become a better football player, you can still be labeled a nonfootball injury by these designations. I actually wish that they would increase the parameters. I don't think a guy that's training to become better should be penalized for getting hurt. But it's a very vague rule that oftentimes the clubs enforce when they know that a player was doing something stupid for the most part.

TRAVIS: Yeah. There have been some horror stories.

JASON: Tons of them.

TRAVIS: It can get pretty bad. But basically you just want to, one, make sure that you're always in shape and not getting yourself into a bad position. But two, also, don't do dangerous shit where you could really fuck your shit up.

JASON: Like we say all the time, you can be dumb. Just don't be too dumb.

TRAVIS: Don't be real dumb.

JASON: Don't be real dumb. I've been real dumb before. It's been close.

JASON
YOU CAN BE DUMB. JUST DON'T BE TOO DUMB.

Where do players go after they get ejected? Do they have to stay in the locker room and just sit there?

92%er: Thomas_lee17 via YouTube

TRAVIS: Well, Jason has only ejected himself from practice. I've actually ejected myself from a game. I've gotten ejected against the Jaguars, I believe, in 2015 or '16.

JASON: When you threw the flag at the ref?

TRAVIS: Yeah, I said some things that the ref didn't like, flagged me for that one. I looked back after I realized he flagged me and had a towel on my hip and threw the towel at him. I was just an asshole. I flagged the ref. That, my friends, will get you ejected. Two flags, two personal misconducts or whatever the fuck it's called.

I was lucky that Nick Foles came through for the boys and won that game because I sat in the training room and watched it on the TV. Sitting there like please, please, Coach Reid is going to fucking kill me already for getting ejected. Please win this game so it doesn't look like I made us lose. But yeah, you get sent to the locker room, and if you're an away team that's probably where you stay. I'm sure you can leave if you're the home team, but I wanted to make sure that I was there when everybody got back in the locker room after the game.

JASON: Yeah, leave it up to Nicky Foles to answer your dreams and prayers. Sure did mine. Did you see that he just won like a pickleball . . . ?

TRAVIS: What can't he do?

JASON: So I saw him this year, I think during training camp, he came up to Philly for something and I ended up having dinner with him. He was telling me that him and [his wife] Tori had gotten really into pickleball. I'm like, "Oh yeah, I had no idea." He was legitimately competing in world events.

TRAVIS: You could tell by the way he flicks a football that he's just saucy.

JASON: He's got that athleticism.

TRAVIS: Dude, he's probably just slicing.

JASON: He's got the length. I mean, his wingspan is freaky.

TRAVIS: He is probably hovering over the kitchen.

JASON: Yeah, good luck getting the ball around.

Before you snap the ball, what is it you're pointing to and yelling about?

92%er: Thomas Mulholland via email

TRAVIS: Every player is out here just fucking . . . "You! You!"

JASON: "You!" So on every offense, the blocking scheme needs to be communicated—depending on the play, and different systems do it differently. There are some systems where the center will point where he's going. There are some systems where the center is pointing out the Mike. There are some systems where the quarterback is pointing out the Mike.

TRAVIS: Those of you that don't know who the Mike [middle linebacker] is, he's the middle of the three linebackers.

JASON: Correct, but Mike can also be just the middle of three birds, because if you have weak rotation, now the Mike is the Will [weak-side linebacker] or the same.

TRAVIS: Anybody. Yeah.

JASON: Anyways, so without going down that rabbit hole, all of the plays in the rulebook have—

TRAVIS: You've said "rabbit hole" about ten times today.

JASON: I'm a big rabbit hole guy. Without going down that gopher hole, every play in the playbook has a set of rules. For instance, "two jet protection." The offensive line is responsible four down in the Will.

TRAVIS
YOU'VE SAID "RABBIT HOLE" ABOUT TEN TIMES TODAY.

JASON
I'M A BIG RABBIT HOLE GUY.

TRAVIS: Classic two jet protection.

JASON: And based on how you're teaching it as an offense, the center might say, hey, Mike is 54. That means we have the next one over from the Mike, which would be the Will. So everybody knows that we're responsible for four down and the Will.

Some offense would just be, hey, just go point the Mike, the Will out. Hey, Will is 36. All right. Then we got the four down in number 36. There are different calls that indicate how you're blocking those guys in pass plays. It could be a sort protection, which means you're responsible for more people than there are blockers.

TRAVIS: Let me write this down . . .

JASON: So if there's three blockers, you're sorting out four potential players. There could be a man protection, which is five-oh. You have all five guys on the line. There's a lot of different things. Anyways, all of this communication is just to set the blocking arrangement so that everybody knows who they're responsible for and you yell it so that everyone hears you.

TRAVIS: 54 is Sam [strong-side linebacker].

JASON: That's it.

TRAVIS: Nice. So you point and yell. So everyone's on the same page. Got it. All right.

How hard is it really to move O-line positions? Like when a right guard moves to the left guard, sometimes announcers act like it's no big deal, but sometimes they act like it's the most impressive thing an NFL player can do. I imagine it's like driving on the other side of the road.

JASON: I would say it's a little bit harder than driving on the other side of the road. Some players are very good and natural at switching sides and are ambidextrous. It's more similar to switch-hitting in baseball, but hitting a baseball is way harder.

What it really comes down to is you're using your feet in a different stance and stagger than you do on the other side of the ball. Maybe more importantly, your hands have to be used differently. Your inside hand placement is obviously with a different hand and that has a lot to do with how you pass set and your relationship with the defender. I would say it is definitely hard, but some guys are very good at it and it's not difficult for them at all. They can go back and forth.

A lot of it is player specific. Some guys are awful when you try and have them play another side. They just can't figure it out quickly and some guys can switch over like it's nothing. That's one of the reasons why backup guys can play both sides and move and play either left or right.

TRAVIS: The tweeners.

JASON: It's a valuable thing to have.

TRAVIS: We had a few of those guys, yeah.

JASON: This always reminds me of the Pro Bowl, back when you actually used to play the game. The biggest issue all week was always that all of the Pro Bowl tackles that made it were always left tackles and somebody had to go play right.

Nobody wanted to play right because like your right leg's back instead of your left, you're using your hands different. They all didn't want to play it and it would devolve into the youngest guy with the least Pro Bowls always had to play right, and he would be getting his ass kicked every game and we'd have to slide it over to him because that was the only problem with the pass rush. So it's definitely a thing. It's definitely hard, but for some guys it's easier than others.

What is on the wristband that the quarterback wears and what is on the massive sheet that the coach holds all game? Looks like a lot of words.

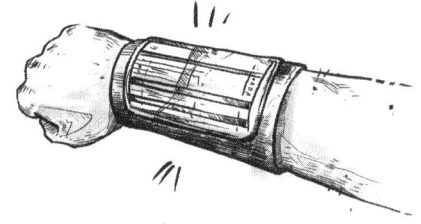

92%er: @hannahmcdougall9182
via YouTube

JASON: It is a lot of words, and it's very confusing.

TRAVIS: It's ironic that you asked what both of those things were because they do have something in common. They have the plays on them. That menu card that you see the coach has, well, that's exactly what it is. It's a list of all the plays that we have separated and organized in a way that the coach can call them according to the situation that's at hand. Whether it be a first down, second down, they have plays specifically in the game plan for their first and second down. That goes with third down, third and short, third and long, meaning third and two versus third and let's say ten-plus.

JASON: I just don't like the layout of the sheets when I see them. I think that I don't really understand them. Maybe if I understood it more and I actually went through it with one of the offensive coordinators, I would get it. But whenever I get it to be like, what's that third down run again? What is it? And then I get it and I have to find the third down. I'm like, why don't you just have this color coordinated? And some of it is color coordinated. I don't know. It's confusing to me.

TRAVIS: It's not confusing at all.

JASON: It's not?

TRAVIS: It's not. It is so labeled and clear-cut. Third down runs is one hundred percent a section in there. You'll see like first, second down runs, goal line runs, short, third and short runs.

JASON: Yeah, but I would think the third down would all be like in the same area so that you don't have to flip to the pass section.

TRAVIS: You just don't like to separate run and pass.

JASON: It feels weird, very segmented, and it's hard.

TRAVIS: It's not.

JASON: So I am curious about the quarterback wristband.

TRAVIS: You never looked at it?

JASON: No.

TRAVIS: Sometimes to get a play call in, it's just easier to say a number. I would assume that's what it's for.

JASON: Yeah, they're usually longer plays where there's like a lot of words.

TRAVIS: I don't know. I think it's different in every room. The wristband is to help the quarterback on whatever he's having trouble with.

JASON: Like, listen, I get that we want to be creative. I'm not a fan of the wristband. If you have to read the play, I feel like there's a zero percent chance we're going to be efficient at this play.

TRAVIS: That is so fucking true. I don't think I've ever seen Pat [Mahomes] look at a wristband.

JASON: I mean, we do it all the time and sometimes it's successful, sometimes it's not.

TRAVIS: Maybe it's because you only get to talk in the microphone up until about fifteen seconds on the play clock. Maybe it's just like a quick way to get to like play 35 instead of trying to having to say—

JASON: Having to say the whole thing?

TRAVIS: Yeah.

JASON: I get it. But I think it should be like this: get the play 35. It should be a look. And then, you know, it's double double right. And if you're going like this and you're like F mode trips right, all this stuff, I'm like, dude.

TRAVIS: I hope you can read the defense faster than that.

JASON: Yeah, dude, I cannot stand when the play call sounds like a short story. He's like F move to trips right. Z shift. Ninety-four, waggle, kill, alert, this.

TRAVIS: You don't like the alerts?

JASON: Yeah. The end.

TRAVIS: Dude, the alerts are home run shots, dude.

JASON: Yeah. The end. I don't like when it starts off "Once upon a time" . . . F mode to trips right, then it's just too much. I feel like if it gets that long, it just needs one word and everybody needs to know what that one word is. What are we running? We're running "freight train right." You know what we're doing.

TRAVIS: Concept. Easy. That's all you had to say. It's freight train right.

JASON: Freight train right. It's got all that built in. Don't get to do all this verbiage. I don't know.

TRAVIS: You do know.

JASON: It's way harder than what I'm making it out to be, especially when guys don't get that rep.

TRAVIS: Basically, there's abbreviated plays on the wristband and all the plays are on the call sheet.

JASON: It's laminated like a Waffle House menu.

TRAVIS: It's not a thousand percent laminated. You can't get that thing wet, man won't be able to read it.

JASON: All right. Well, that was good.

TRAVIS: That's a solid question. And now I know that I can read a fucking chart better than Jason.

JASON: For sure. I can't. I look at that thing. I'm like, okay, what are the first and second down runs we're trying to get to this drive? That's all I give a fuck about.

TRAVIS: It says it right there. And you're hilarious.

What is a piece of your uniform you are required to wear that you feel has no purpose and you would play . . . ?

92%er: @ms_katedavis14 via X

JASON: Thigh pads and kneepads. Thigh pads and kneepads. Thigh pads and kneepads.

TRAVIS: I couldn't even finish the sentence there. No, I love wearing thigh pads and kneepads because that's typically where I'm getting tackled. So I'm definitely wearing those. And I'm not fucking wearing the little tiny kneepads neither. I'm wearing them big old things because I got big knees. Make sure I stay protected out there. Always protect yourselves. Know what I'm saying? Mama always taught me that.

TRAVIS
MAKE SURE I STAY PROTECTED OUT THERE. ALWAYS PROTECT YOURSELVES. KNOW WHAT I'M SAYING? MAMA ALWAYS TAUGHT ME THAT.

6

Hockey

Who would you guys think would make the best hockey lineup using NFL stars?

92%er: @user-bx7fm4iy2d via YouTube

JASON: So let's do starting five, right? We can't do a whole hockey team. So we're doing starting five and a goalie. Start writing some down.

TRAVIS: Do you have a pen and paper over there or something? What do you write?

JASON: Yeah, we always got to take notes. Travis, so we got defense.

TRAVIS: What are you writing down? You doodling right now?

JASON: Are we current or former players? Or all the above?

TRAVIS: I say all the above.

JASON: So any player in history?

TRAVIS: Yep.

JASON: Okay, I think I'm going to go more modern.

TRAVIS: I'm just going to go for the guys that I know that can skate. So at center, are we allowed to pick us?

JASON: Oh, I think we avoid us. I think we don't pick us.

TRAVIS: All right.

JASON: Are you going to pick me or . . . ?

TRAVIS: One hundred percent I was going to pick you.

JASON: Oh, thank you.

TRAVIS: But now I'm not.

JASON: Okay, for the sake of the question, everyone could skate. Although my first pick was going to be JJ Watt, just because I know he can skate.

TRAVIS: I was going to go the Watt brothers and then me and you and then just put Gronk [Rob Gronkowski] at goalie because I saw him at goalie.

JASON: Wait, at goalie you saw Gronk?

TRAVIS: Yeah, he did something with the Tampa Bay Lightning and he was in net for a practice or something like that.

JASON: How did it work?

TRAVIS: It was a great bit. I enjoyed watching it. I don't know if any of us in net against actual NHL players is going to look good. But Gronk made it look as fun as it possibly could. Kind of got jealous. I want to do it now. I want to hit up the Blackhawks and get in net or something.

JASON: I'm going at center. I'm going JJ Watt because I feel like he's an Eric Lindros–type power player. He's going to back-check hard. He's going to play a physical game in front of the net.

TRAVIS: Team guy, one hundred percent.

JASON: Yeah, I mean, you're not going to find somebody that hustles like that.

TRAVIS: He's not going to play his gap. Know what I mean?

JASON: Exactly. He's got a little creativeness to him. Left wing, going with speed. I need some speed. If JJ Watt is holding down the center position, I need speed—going Tyreek Hill. He's going to fly up and down.

TRAVIS: If we're assuming everyone can skate . . . this is like the rookie that the Blackhawks just got, I was talking about. [Connor] Bedard? I just know I love watching that dude play hockey. So who else we got?

JASON: I'm going right wing. I got to have a left-handed person because they need to be able to cut to the middle, get a good angle on the net. Mike Vick.

TRAVIS: All right. Yeah. I mean, fuck, you guys are a fast, powerful team right now. Who we got playing defense?

JASON: Defense, I feel like it's got to be two linebackers that were beasts. I'm going to go Dick Butkus and Ray Lewis to just bring that energy.

TRAVIS: Dick Butkus . . .

JASON: Just going to bring that energy. Dick Butkus, a lot of toughness.

TRAVIS: Dick Butkus played tight end, I thought.

JASON: No, Dick Butkus played defense, middle linebacker.

TRAVIS: Who am I thinking of?

JASON: You're thinking of the other Bears coach. Mike Ditka.

TRAVIS: Sorry, Mike. You're a legend.

JASON: You're getting your dicks mixed up. What are you doing here, bud?

JASON

YOU'RE GETTING YOUR DICKS MIXED UP.

TRAVIS: Fuck. I hate it when I get them shuffled around.

JASON: And then a goalie because I don't know if anybody can play goalie. Usually, goaltenders are really skinny, so they're agile and can move. I don't think any NFL player is going to be able to do that well. So I'm going to go the opposite direction, which is what every youth team does, where they just put somebody who occupies a lot of space. I'm going to go Tony Siragusa. Rest in peace. He's also going to bring good energy.

TRAVIS: Your goalie needs to bring the fucking energy.

One of the Utah NHL team name choices is the Yeti. How do you guys feel about the list of names and what would you like the new NHL team name to be called?

92%er: Rambleonrosa36 via Club 92

TRAVIS: "Yetis" is pretty fucking cool. I think it is a great name for Utah, knowing that they're up in the mountains over there. And they probably had a few Yeti sightings here and there.

JASON: Utah Yeti? The one thing I don't like is that it's not plural. When I think of animal names, they're always plural names. I've never heard of an animal singular name. Like it should be like the "Yetis," right? Or are they doing it like "Octopi," where "Yeti" is a plural form of "Yet"?

TRAVIS: "Cacti." Yeah. That's a good point.

JASON: I think it should be the Utah Yetis if they're going for it.

TRAVIS: I do love the Yetis or the Yeti, the Utah Yeti. You're right, though. It does sound like it needs an *S*.

JASON: It needs to be "Yetis." It's wrong. It's Utah Yetis. It's not the Chicago Bear. It's not the Philadelphia Eagle. It needs to be the Utah Yetis.

TRAVIS: What's the other word for "Yeti"?

JASON: "The Sasquatch."

TRAVIS: The Utah Sasquatch?

JASON: "Abominable Snowmen." You can do that.

TRAVIS: That's a long-ass fucking name though. The options to choose from are the Frost, the Utah Ice, Utah Powder, the Utah Mountaineers. Don't love it. The Utah Freeze.

JASON: I like "Mountaineers." "Powder" is weak. "Powder" reminds me of a . . . what was that movie with a really pasty white guy?

TRAVIS: It's called *Powder*. That was a terrifying movie. It has a place in my mind that I don't love.

JASON: Yeah. You can't forget it.

TRAVIS: Fuck bullying. Black Diamonds, the Utah Black Diamonds. Don't love that. The Utah Blast, the Utah Caribou, the Utah Blizzard Swarm, the Utah Swarm, the Utah Hive, Outlaws, Getty . . . the Squall?

JASON: Squall.

TRAVIS: Squall, the Fury, the Glaciers, Canyons . . . Utah Canyons? It's got a kind of a ring to it. It doesn't strike fear in anybody though. The Utah Venom. Why would it be that? And "HC," which stands for "Hockey Club." That is so wack.

JASON: Get that weak shit out of here. Don't start doing this bullshit "FC" stuff in hockey. I'm out on that.

TRAVIS: I'm out on that too.

JASON: Hockey has got some of the best mascots and jersey designs out there. Don't start bringing this "HC" bullshit.

TRAVIS: Not just *some* of the best: *the* best. Literally the best. Out of these, who are you going with? I like one specific.

JASON: Well, first of all, I love the Utah Yetis. I think that's a great name.

TRAVIS: It's a good ring, yeah. I think it's a little childish for a hockey team. I like the Utah Outlaws.

JASON: Outlaws? I don't like it because I don't know that has anything to do with Utah. I guess it does because it's part of the West. But when I think of Utah, I think of Mormons. I think of the opposite of outlaws. I think about pretty much the most law-abiding citizens on the planet when I think of Utah.

TRAVIS: You must not know.

JASON: I must not know. Outlaws, right next to all those jazz players in Utah. I kinda dig Utah Frost or Utah Ice. I see what they're going for with those.

TRAVIS: It's just so simple though.

JASON: "Blizzard" is pretty good. "Squall" is too weak. It can't be a winter squall. Glaciers, Utah Glaciers, Glacier National Park, I think, is partly in Utah and Montana.

TRAVIS: What do you think of the Mammoths, the Utah Mammoths?

JASON: I mean, I dig it.

TRAVIS: It's too hard to put an *S* on the end of a *TH*, though. "Mammoths."

JASON: The Utah Mammoths. It feels weird when these are all singular. When I think of an animal, it needs to be plural. I don't know why. It doesn't fit in my brain being a singular animal.

TRAVIS: Utah, I think you guys just got to keep digging. I don't love any of these. I'm kind of on board with "Yeti" and "Outlaws."

JASON: I'm on board with "Yetis." Ooh, how about we combine two? The Utah Ice Outlaws! I can get behind that now.

Which hockey players, past or present, do you think could play in the NFL and at what position?

92%er: Debb13m via Club 92

JASON: Eric Lindros could play in the NFL.

TRAVIS: Yeah, he was a big dude.

JASON: I feel pretty confident about that one.

TRAVIS: You think he's a tight end?

JASON: Dude, so he came to the golf outing we had for (Be)Philly this year. He's massive, man. He could have put on weight easily and played O-line. He definitely could have played tight end for what his stature was during a player.

TRAVIS: He's rocking jersey number 88. Come on, he's a tight end.

JASON: Who else? Freaking [Jaromír] Jágr with this freaking mullet would have been awesome to watch out there on a football field.

TRAVIS: I don't know what position he's playing, but I'm with you. You think Claude Giroux could have found his way as a wide receiver or something?

JASON: I don't know. Maybe. I mean, he's feisty.

TRAVIS: That's what I'm saying. Maybe DB?

JASON: I don't know. DB's tough. Maybe safety. He used to come in and ask to arm-wrestle anybody. He's just one of them type of guys. So mentality-wise, yes, absolutely could play in the NFL. Physically, I'm going to have to see that.

TRAVIS: What about some of the bruisers from the league? What's his name playing for the fucking Leafs?

JASON: I always think of Zdeno Chara.

TRAVIS: Oh, Chara, the six-foot-eleven defender from Boston? He could play D-end.

JASON: I think he'd be a D-end. Got that reach. He's got some wiggle to him. He can put some weight on, play some offensive tackle.

TRAVIS: There you go.

JASON: That's what I mean, defenseman. Just keep the guy in front of you. He's got that skill.

TRAVIS: You think a guy like [Connor] McDavid, who's the fastest thing on fucking ice, can play receiver or running back? He weaves like a running back when he's on the ice. It's sweet.

JASON: He's got the elusiveness, but it's hard.

TRAVIS: He's got the vision for running back.

JASON: It's just hard to gauge because skating is so . . . I've seen guys that skate incredibly well, and then you see them run on a field and it's just not the same. Not that they're unathletic, but it's an entirely different muscle group that you're activating ice skating than you are when you're actually running. But the elusiveness is there. The twitch is there. Maybe.

TRAVIS: Past or present? Is Wayne Gretzky finding his way on the NFL football field?

JASON: I don't think so. As much as I love Wayne . . .

TRAVIS: You don't think Wayne's in there?

JASON: You know, greatness is greatness. So probably we would figure it out. But he never struck me as like having speed or—

TRAVIS: Have you ever seen him race? They did like crossover, it was him and like three other professional athletes, I think.

JASON: You're right. And they did a hundred-meter dash. Yes!

TRAVIS: And he fucking smoked everybody.

JASON: He smoked 'em. You're right.

TRAVIS: He was rolling. You know he was a two-sport athlete.

JASON: He was a great baseball player.

TRAVIS: I'm pretty sure he got drafted by the Expos, yeah.

JASON: You know what? I must say he could have done it.

PART 3

OUR
MUSINGS

7

Education

I'm a longtime Philly teacher, about to start my 30th year tomorrow. Who were your favorite teachers and why?

92%er: Tara Shaw-Caruso (@TShawCaruso) via X

JASON: Well, first of all, Tara, thank you so much for the service you are providing. Can't say enough good things about teachers.

TRAVIS: I've had some great ones, man. It's going to be hard to just list one.

JASON: Were you in any AP classes? In high school?

TRAVIS: No. What the fuck? No.

JASON: You're in nature studies?

TRAVIS: No, I couldn't have—

JASON: With Mr. Baxson?

TRAVIS: Dad always said if I just applied myself, I could have done way better.

JASON: There's no question about that.

TRAVIS: Jason wins that. He was in all AP classes, as well as he was in music, as well as he was in swim cadets.

JASON: Swim cadets was, I don't know . . . I wasn't *in* swim cadets.

TRAVIS: Tell everybody what swim cadets was.

JASON: It's our synchronized swimming team at Cleveland Heights High School.

TRAVIS: The Heights, baby.

JASON: That's right. And swim cadets would put a show on every year and they would choose certain men from their grades. And I was one of the chosen people to be a part of the show.

TRAVIS: Don't say they *chose*, you *volunteered*.

JASON: No, they chose. They said, "You're funny. We think you'd be a good addition to the show." And I made a fool of myself and made the show.

TRAVIS: Didn't you have like a sax, like a solo saxophone act on the diving board or something?

JASON: Nope, I don't think that sounds right.

TRAVIS: Dude, I *swear* I remember seeing you on the diving board.

JASON: There's no saxophone on the diving board. I honestly cannot remember what happened. There's footage somewhere out there. It was definitely recorded. Who was your favorite teacher at, in the Cleveland Heights University Heights School District? It's tough!

TRAVIS: There are some great ones that come to mind.

JASON: Should we start at Fairfax Elementary? Is that where we want to start? If we're going Fairfax, I'm going Mr. Ione.

TRAVIS: I didn't even have Mr. Ione, and I loved Mr. Ione.

JASON: That's because everyone loved Mr. Ione.

TRAVIS

DIDN'T YOU HAVE LIKE A SAX, LIKE A SOLO SAXOPHONE ACT ON THE DIVING BOARD OR SOMETHING?

JASON

NOPE, I DON'T THINK THAT SOUNDS RIGHT.

TRAVIS: He was just one of the coolest guys.

JASON: Word of mouth about Mr. Ione traveled. We used to play this game where it was a spelling game. And if you spell, I forget how you even play, but if you spelled the word correctly or something like that, you got to shoot the eraser at the wastebasket. And then there was a whole point scoring system. And that was a whole thing.

TRAVIS: Bring sports into learning. That's going to get the Kelces every time.

JASON: Everybody loved it.

TRAVIS: That class was sweet, we were doing sports with education.

JASON: I'm trying to remember who the fifth-grade teacher I had was, and you would always get a whole pack of fuzzy balls.

TRAVIS: Oh my gosh, Mrs. . . . . Ah, this is going to kill me. She was the nicest lady in the world, too. I actually had her.

JASON: Yeah, Mrs. . . . .

TRAVIS: Something with an *M*.

JASON: *M*? Mrs. . . . . we got to text Mom. Mom would know.

TRAVIS: I'm going to go with Mr. Campbell. It was my kindergarten teacher. He ended up being my basketball coach in fourth and fifth grade, or fifth and sixth grade.

JASON: Yeah, I didn't do kindergarten in Cleveland Heights. I don't even re-member. Dude, you know who I didn't like? You know who was terrible? Mrs. Schwartz. And she was pretty much the same way her name sounded. She was mean as hell. For some reason, it always reminded me of the word "warts," and she was just a mean lady. She did not take any shit.

TRAVIS: "Jason, sit down."

JASON: She was Mrs. Schwartz. Everybody didn't like her.

TRAVIS: She had no candy. She didn't have a candy jar. That's what it was. All the elementary school teachers, if you have candy jars, you are a fan favorite.

JASON: Hopefully, you're not like Mrs. Schwartz, Tara. Hopefully, you're not like Mrs. Schwartz.

TRAVIS: Shout-out to Mrs. Schwartz, because I don't want to bash anybody.

JASON: Well, I mean, listen, I'm all for being mean to kids. Growing up, I was anti–Mrs. Schwartz. Now, I'm definitely pro–Mrs. Schwartz.

TRAVIS: You got a little Mrs. Schwartz in you?

JASON: These kids are too . . . if it was up to me—

TRAVIS: Too soft.

JASON: One of the things that always used to be intimidating is when we showed up to school and Dad gave the teachers permission to hit us.

TRAVIS: One thing, just whack them right upside the head.

JASON: "No, you can hit them if you want. I promise you, I'm more than okay with that. They deserve it."

TRAVIS: Never got hit. Never got hit. They don't hit kids in the Cleveland Heights school system.

JASON: But I can guarantee you, Dad would have been fine with that.

TRAVIS: One hundred percent. He was bargaining for it. One of my favorite teachers of all time, and we actually ended up going to college with his sons, Mr. Thaxton.

JASON: Oh, you can't leave out Mr. Thaxton.

TRAVIS: Cleveland Heights science teacher. He actually taught me—

JASON: ZZ Top–esque beard.

TRAVIS: He was just a cool cat, man. One of my favorite guys of all time.

JASON: He was an iconic Cleveland Heights teacher.

TRAVIS: I think he grew garlic out in Hudson on the side. Yeah, that's awesome, man. Mr. Thaxton.

JASON: I actually went to the barn where they had all the garlic growing because I was back home with Jake, his son, when he went to Cincinnati with us, but great family.

TRAVIS: I used to love Nature Studies because we would actually learn about the trees and the birds and everything and the insects.

JASON: Tell me about these trees.

TRAVIS: That are around—

JASON: Tell me about these trees.

TRAVIS: —the Cleveland Heights schools.

JASON: What did you learn about the trees, Travis? I'm waiting for the trees.

TRAVIS: So we would, some days, we would take Nature Study walks—

JASON: I know. Very aware.

TRAVIS: And we would walk around the school and we would learn about everything. I've actually seen Mr. Thaxton eat a few bugs.

JASON: If I'm going high school . . . Mr. Javorik was middle school. Mrs. Bukovec was Heights High. I can't leave out my band teacher, Mr. Brett Baker, one of the few teachers I still keep in touch with.

TRAVIS: Miss O'Keefe at Heights.

JASON: That doesn't ring a bell for me.

TRAVIS: There are a lot of teachers. Coach Robbo and Coach Mike Jones, baby.

JASON: Well, that's where I was going to go next was Coach Robbo, Coach Mike Jones, and Coach *[unintelligible]*.

TRAVIS: Some of our favorite guys of all time.

JASON: All health and PE. I learned everything I know about drugs, human anatomy, sex, from my football coaches, which I don't know if that's good. I feel like that's a pretty one-sided demographic there, but I think they did a good job.

TRAVIS: You're killing it. You're absolutely killing it. Look at you. You're a professional athlete and you got three baby girls. You're absolutely killing it in the health department.

JASON: All seriousness. We grew up in a wonderful school district with a lot of great teachers.

TRAVIS: A bunch of them.

JASON: I would not trade that for anything in the world. So, you know, keep doing your thing, Tara Shaw-Caruso. The world needs more teachers. So we appreciate you.

What college would you have gone to if Cincinnati hadn't been a choice?

92%er: @tjwiscott via YouTube

TRAVIS: It's actually a decent question. Jason, weren't you about to go Ivy League to play saxophone?

JASON: No.

TRAVIS: Right?

JASON: You keep saying that. No, I was not. I could not have gotten into Ivy League. I was thinking about Colgate University. But at the time when I chose Cincinnati, I narrowed it down to Pittsburgh, UC [University of Cincinnati], or Ohio State. I was going to be a walk-on at any three of them.

I felt like Ohio State was going to be an uphill battle to earn a scholarship. A lot of talent there, a lot of really good players. So it came down to Pittsburgh and Cincinnati. I really liked Pittsburgh for the majority of the recruiting process. And then for some reason, when I went to Cincinnati—I physically went to the university—I fell in love with the campus, all the coaches, all the players. It just seemed like the spot. So I ended up going there.

TRAVIS: Nice. Well, I was Cincinnati through and through. Basically, I went to the University of Cincinnati for a basketball camp and visited Jason the rest of that weekend, stayed with him in the dorm, hung out with him, got to meet everybody on the team, and also got to meet a few of the coaches at one of the spring ball practices that Jason was having. And sure enough, I walked out of Cincinnati with a scholarship that weekend. Paul Longo, the strength guy, asked for my highlight tape. And Big Ed Kelce made sure that I didn't go to Cincinnati without it.

JASON: Paul came up to me in the weight room when he found out you were coming up to campus. He's like, "Nobody even knew who your brother was. I'm like, guys, this is Jason's brother. He's probably got some pretty good genes." I forget how he phrased it, but he came up to me. He's like, "I looked at the kid's highlight tape. I'm like, what are we doing, guys? Offer the kid a scholarship." He was amazed that it hadn't happened already.

TRAVIS: Well, two and eight the year before at Cleveland Heights.

JASON: Not a lot of eyes on the tape?

TRAVIS: Probably.

JASON: Yeah. Yeah.

TRAVIS: So that being said, I think after my junior year, at least going into my senior year, I was already committed to be a Bearcat.

JASON: Paul switched my position. And he's the reason you got a scholarship to Cincinnati.

TRAVIS: As a quarterback.

JASON: Shout-out to the old strength coach, man, Paul Longo.

TRAVIS: Doggone. Legend. Absolute legend. To finish off the story, it was really down to if I went the football route, I was probably going to go Cincinnati or I think it was UNC. I think North Carolina.

JASON: No, no, no. West Virginia was the one that you really wanted to go to.

TRAVIS: West Virginia was where I wanted to play basketball. I wanted to play for Coach Bob Huggins, the legendary Huggy Bear, the Cincinnati Bearcat legend. He actually played at West Virginia University, then coached there for such a long time. But he had just moved there from being a head coach at Kansas State. So he honored a few of the scholarships that they had already given out. And it was kind of up in the air. I'm not even sure if I would have went there if I had a full scholarship the first year.

And yeah, I went to Dad. I was like, "Man, I really want to play basketball at West Virginia under Hugs." He's like, "You're a man of your fucking word. You don't go back on your word. You already committed. Don't be like these other guys who just fucking—" Now look at everybody in college football.

JASON: Oh, it's so crazy, looking back. That's the way Dad was, though.

TRAVIS: I appreciate my dad for keeping me honest about my word.

JASON: Even though the colleges will go back on their word in a second.

TRAVIS: In a fucking heartbeat. Now it's the Wild Wild West and it's a fucking free-for-all.

JASON: It's crazy. Yeah, it's nuts now.

TRAVIS: I was almost a Mountaineer. It was almost down there. Tar Heel. But proud Bearcat, baby.

8

Movies and TV

Who plays Travis and Jason in a Lifetime movie?

JASON: First off, do we deserve a Lifetime movie?

TRAVIS: Man, I feel like Mom might deserve a Lifetime movie more than us.

JASON: Yeah, Mom and Dad. I'm kind of with you on that. I guess we'd be in it, though, so we still got to cast ourselves.

TRAVIS: Yeah, we do. We also need to cast Ed and Donna.

JASON: Oh, yeah. Great point. Well, who do you think would be the blockbuster actors to play us? I think all week, the big comparison was *Step Brothers*. Obviously, John C. Reilly, Will Ferrell. I think that would be great.

TRAVIS: I'd be honored. I'd watch it.

JASON: I kind of want that to happen just so I could meet John C. Reilly, because you met him. You were in a show with him.

TRAVIS: *Moonbase 8.* These guys are unbelievable. Fred Armisen, Tim Heidecker, John C. Reilly. When I tell you it was an all-star cast, the guys that have been doing it since they were kids, they just had an unbelievable ability to hit every single scene perfectly.

When we did the scene over, nothing was said the same as it was the first take because they know they got that good take already. And here I am, the freaking jamoke in the room, trying to figure out when my line is, exactly how to say it. But damn, it was an unbelievable experience.

JASON: It was cool seeing you on the TV.

TRAVIS: It was arguably almost cooler off camera, because those three are like best friends. They're singing Beatles together on an acoustic guitar. John C. Reilly's just harmonizing. I was being entertained in the middle of trying to be entertainment. Dude, it was awesome. And it's a hilarious show if you guys are into comedy scripts.

JASON: I think that would obviously be a great cast based on a previous role. But they don't really look like it. So we're going for looks. I got to say, you, the basketball player . . .

TRAVIS: Jonas? Jonas Valančiūnas?

JASON: Yeah. I mean, you guys look just like each other.

TRAVIS: I've been trying to get a picture with this guy.

JASON: He's big-time.

TRAVIS: I will say this: When I saw Jonas Valančiūnas get drafted to the Raptors back in 2008, I immediately realized we're Lithuanian because I felt like they just slapped my picture on the screen and said this guy got drafted. But Jonas Valančiūnas for me, and then it would have to be who? Bert Kreischer?

JASON: *2 Bears, 1 Cave.* Yeah, I'll take that. Bert's a funny guy. He would nail the part, I'm sure. I always love *East Bound and Down.* I try and replicate Danny McBride a little bit in my comedy.

TRAVIS: I can see that.

JASON: Always been a big Danny McBride fan. Certainly the year I had the mullet, it would have been a really good casting for that. Everybody always says I look like Zach Galifianakis, which I don't know if you know this, but if you're white and have a beard, every other white dude with a long beard looks just like you. So, Zach Galifianakis, we're the same.

TRAVIS: I'm thinking more like Jack Black. You guys have the same delivery almost in some manner.

JASON: They asked me who would be my choice for halftime show at the Super Bowl, and I without question said Tenacious D.

TRAVIS: Tenacious D?

JASON: You can't tell me that would not be a killer.

TRAVIS: They're not getting everybody hype, but I'd enjoy it. That's for damn sure. I got asked this actually during the media day, what actor would play you in a movie? I said Channing Tatum because I got a lot of Channing Tatum references when I was in high school when I had the baby face and the low buzz cut.

JASON: Channing Tatum is not playing me. I don't know what you're talking about.

TRAVIS: No, he's playing me. I got a lot of those comparisons when I was a kid, especially when it was like *Coach Carter*, him being the only white guy on the team, me always being the only white guy on every basketball team I was on. But yeah, I think they said Liam Hemsworth. So would the Hemsworth brothers play us?

JASON: I guess when Thor was kind of fat and had the beard, the one Marvel movie where he was kind of out of shape, he kind of did look like me. I don't know. Sure. Who's playing Mom and Dad?

TRAVIS: That's a good one right there. Who's the woman that played in *Home Alone*? I don't know her name, but I always thought that was Mom.

JASON: Catherine O'Hara.

TRAVIS: Shout-out to Catherine. She's obviously in way more movies than just *Home Alone*. Who's playing Dad? There's only one answer.

JASON: I'm not good.

TRAVIS: There's only one answer. Are you kidding me?

JASON: Who, Steven Seagal?

TRAVIS: That's fucking hilarious. He's way too in shape, but I don't even know if that's a good way to describe Steven Seagal.

JASON: Steven Seagal is not in shape. That's what I'm saying.

TRAVIS: No, but that's the thing. That's what I'm saying. He's way too in shape to be Dad. We gotta go more like John Candy or John Goodman.

JASON: Dude, John Goodman's like my favorite actor of all time. John Goodman and Jeff Bridges, which explains why I like *The Big Lebowski* so much. The Dude. There were a lot of people saying that Dad sounded like Jeff Bridges. And he would certainly be honored to be played by the Dude.

TRAVIS: *The Big Lebowski*, one of the most popular movies about absolutely nothing.

JASON: Who's playing Andy Reid? Eric Stonestreet, right?

TRAVIS: Ooh, Stonestreet, he's got the voice. He already plays Randy Reid in the skit with the Chiefs. And he'd kill it. Ooh, you know who else would be a good one? Al Bundy himself.

JASON: Al Bundy to be Andy Reid?

TRAVIS: Big Ed, yeah.

JASON: Oh, Big Ed, just from a purely similar parenting style.

TRAVIS: My guy, Ed O'Neill, man. He could definitely play Ed Kelce in a movie. He'd have to wear a body suit, but he could play it for sure.

JASON: Yeah, he's a professional. Nick Sirianni, Doug Pederson.

TRAVIS: Sirianni. I could see like a Ben Affleck playing Sirianni.

JASON: I mean, Ben Affleck's talented.

JASON: What about Dougie P?

TRAVIS: Who would be Doug P?

JASON: Sam Elliott?

TRAVIS: No. I was thinking more the lines of Matthew McConaughey.

JASON: Oh, that'd be good. That'd be real good.

If you could have been on any team from kids' movies or TV show, which would it be and why?

92%er: @ValerieBarbian via X

JASON: Let's think kids' movies that are sports teams. *Space Jam*? I mean, kids be on the Monstars. Would you be on the Monstars or would you be on Jordan's Tune Squad? I might go Monstars. That would be a fucking electric group to be a part of.

TRAVIS: Except that you wouldn't be the one controlling your Monstar.

JASON: I might be a Monstar if I'm on the Monstars.

TRAVIS: You're going to be one of those little fuckers? That's who you want to be?

JASON: Not when I steal. Whose talent would I steal? I would steal Shaquille O'Neal's talent.

TRAVIS: Damn. You would.

JASON: That's right. Who the fuck is stopping me with Shaquille O'Neal's talent?

TRAVIS: I don't know. Gregg Popovich?

JASON: Tim Duncan.

TRAVIS: Yeah. Shaq was unstoppable, wasn't he? Stopping him was impossible.

JASON: All right. I think I'm going *Space Jam*. Who are you going?

TRAVIS: I'm going to go . . . man, it was just . . . as a kid, I just loved *Major League*, man.

JASON: That's not a kid's movie.

TRAVIS: It is in my book. Willie Mays Hayes. *Rookie of the Year*. There's so many good ones. *Angels in the Outfield. Kicking & Screaming.* God damn, these are all fucking golden. I'm going to say *Little Giants*.

JASON: Yeah, I figured that's where you're going to go.

TRAVIS: We'd be fucking unstoppable out there. Spike would have no fucking choice but to eat shit.

JASON: I'm taking you against Spike any day.

Favorite Christmas movie? And also, is *Die Hard* a Christmas movie or not?

92%er: Groovygirl858 via Club 92

JASON: So where are we going first? Are we going Christmas movie or *Die Hard* first?

TRAVIS: We got to just knock *Die Hard* out. *Die Hard*'s not a Christmas movie.

JASON: I mean, it's a movie you should watch around Christmas.

TRAVIS: Well, what's the difference?

JASON: It's not a "Christmas spirit" movie. I wouldn't say it's a Christmas movie because you can watch it at any time of the year. *Die Hard* is acceptable to watch anytime.

TRAVIS: Correct.

JASON: You can't watch *Christmas Story* in, you know, March.

TRAVIS: You cannot watch that shit in July.

JASON: But *Die Hard*, you can watch that whenever you want. You can definitely watch it during Christmas and enjoy it because it's a fantastic movie. Actually, I need to watch it again. I have not seen *Die Hard* in a very long time.

TRAVIS: Just picture Bruce Willis walking out of an exploding building with explosions going off and he's just barely alive. That's the whole movie.

JASON: Fair enough.

TRAVIS: He kills it. They did make five of them of him doing that exact thing.

JASON: What is your favorite Christmas movie?

TRAVIS: Damn, man. So many good ones. I mean, *Christmas Story* hits home. That's the one that gives me the feels because it's filmed in Cleveland. Tower City as a kid, I remember going down that slide. On top of that, just like the scene of the outside reminds me of a Cleveland snowy Christmas. I just get the feels from that one.

I'm a comedy guy. I don't like not-funny Christmas movies. So I'm probably gonna say either *Elf* or *Four Christmases*.

JASON: Dude, I love both of those movies. I think I probably put *Elf* above *Four Christmases*, but I'm such a Vince Vaughn guy that I'd watch *Four Christmases* any day of the week. I'm trying to remember. They're all named after the cities they were conceived in or whatever.

TRAVIS: It is classic.

JASON: I think *Christmas Story* is the answer. But *Elf, Four Christmases*.

TRAVIS: *The Grinch* is another good one.

JASON: Gosh, how did we forget about that?

TRAVIS: Jim Carrey is just my favorite in everything, man.

JASON: I watched the original, too. I like the original Grinch. I like any version of it, except the most recent one. My kids like it, so we watch it a lot. But God, *Christmas Vacation*. Man, we are forgetting all of the good ones.

TRAVIS: *Christmas Vacation* is good.

JASON: When's the last time you saw *Christmas Vacation*?

TRAVIS: Probably last Christmas.

JASON: No way you watched it last Christmas.

TRAVIS: I definitely watched it. I love Chevy Chase. I just like *Vegas Vacation* so much more that I can see it on Christmas.

JASON: I think *Christmas Vacation* is the best one. But I didn't really appreciate it when I was younger because I think I didn't get a lot of the humor. It's so much better as an adult. *Christmas Vacation* is great. *Home Alone* is another one like—

TRAVIS: I love it. I can't say anything bad about it. If you put it on, I'll watch it right now. But in terms of my favorites, I just like a little bit more comedy.

JASON: *Jingle All the Way*. You can't go wrong with [Arnold] Schwarzenegger. There's never been a Schwarzenegger movie that I have not enjoyed watching.

TRAVIS: You got me there.

JASON: There's something about the guy.

Why doesn't anyone in the NFL do the Annexation of Puerto Rico play from *Little Giants*?

TRAVIS: I'll let you know right now that it is arguably the worst play that you could ever run in an actual football game. It works so perfect because they were kids and it was a movie. There's no fucking way in hell. I have seen it done in college games, and I don't think it ended up being a game-winning touchdown, but it did get some yards.

JASON: Can we? I don't remember what the play is . . .

TRAVIS: They put the ball on the ground, act like it's a toss. And then somebody else picks it up . . .

JASON: The center sits on it like he doesn't see where it's at.

TRAVIS: Something like that.

JASON: I got to see if it's a legal play.

TRAVIS: It is a legal play for sure. Okay. Maybe. I'm not sure if the center actually—

JASON: It has to actually be possessed by the quarterback for it to count as a legal snap.

TRAVIS: Some of these trick plays, like the Annexation of Puerto Rico or a reverse pass or a funky formation. It's the NFL. Guys aren't getting fucking tricked.

JASON: I mean, guys get tricked all the time, Travis.

TRAVIS: I don't know, man.

JASON: That's like . . . you're a flanker. Your entire career has been tricking people.

TRAVIS: Nope. Not like that.

JASON: Well, I think Travis is on to something. It's probably not a play that's going to work very well in the NFL. Fun to watch in a movie.

JASON

IT'S PROBABLY NOT A PLAY THAT'S GOING TO WORK VERY WELL IN THE NFL. FUN TO WATCH IN A MOVIE.

9

Fashion and Self-Care

What happened to the jockstrap? Seriously, I don't think you boys wear 'em anymore. You just see everything hanging and moving and running, and oh my goodness. Oh my goodness. What happened to the jockstrap?

TRAVIS: Not as aware as this woman at what's going on with the genitals throughout the game, but you know, watch the game for whatever you watch the game for. I'm not here to judge why someone's watching the game and whether or not they're checking out which guy's got what jockstraps on.

JASON: What happened to the jockstrap is they invented compression shorts, and they're just way more efficient at holding everything in place.

TRAVIS: And it eliminates the chafing. So it's like you knock out two birds with one stone. You could just throw on some compression shorts.

JASON: I still wore the jockstrap. There's something I liked about the jockstrap. I only wore it on game day, though. And I would walk around the locker room making my preworkout in nothing but my jockstrap, and I thought it was funny. So maybe that's the reason I wore it, but . . . I also thought it cupped my butt cheek nice and it made my butt look better.

TRAVIS: I didn't realize you were going for a nice look.

JASON: I needed help because I don't have a great ass.

TRAVIS: All right, there you go. The compression shorts came in.

JASON: Yeah, they're a little bit better at doing the job.

TRAVIS: Also, not a lot of guys wear cups anymore and the jockstrap was initially to hold the cup.

JASON: Well, that's how we always used it, but I do think the jockstrap was also utilized before compression shorts to hold the junk. But once you have compression shorts, you didn't need that.

TRAVIS: Glad we could help you out.

JASON: By the way, get your mind out of it. What was that woman's name? Do we remember?

TRAVIS: No, she just said Merry Christmas.

JASON: Merry Christmas to *you*. Just watch some football. She's acting like she's not happy about it.

TRAVIS: "It's so disturbing seeing everybody's junk just jump around on the TV."

JASON: "All of this phallic meat bouncing from thigh to thigh."

If Travis is "El Travador" when he has the mustache, what is his name when he has the playoff beard?

92%er: @AshleyG193 via X

TRAVIS: Ooh, the playoff beard. I go more like . . .

JASON: Nordic?

TRAVIS: Celtic.

JASON: Celtic! I was thinking more Viking.

TRAVIS: What did I say?

JASON: Celtic. Well, I mean, listen, Irish people have beards too. I feel like yours, I think it might be "Red Beard."

TRAVIS: It's not that red.

JASON: Because in the playoff mode, especially, there's like an anger that you play with.

TRAVIS: It's not that red.

JASON: It's a little red. It's got some tinge to it.

TRAVIS: No, you're trying to give me more than what I got.

JASON: I'm not trying to get you, I'm trying to give you . . .

TRAVIS: It's brown.

JASON: I think "Red Beard" is great. It's not "Black Beard." I don't think it's "Brown Beard." I think it's "Red Beard."

TRAVIS: It's definitely "Brown Beard."

JASON: It's "Red Beard."

TRAVIS: It's not "Red Beard."

JASON: If somebody saw that beard and they were like, "Give it a color," they would say "Red beard."

TRAVIS: No, they would not.

JASON: Brandon, come in here. What would you call that beard? Not like the actual color, but if you were going to nickname that beard.

INTERN BRANDON: Let me get in. Travis, get a little closer.

TRAVIS: No.

INTERN BRANDON: Come on.

TRAVIS: You get what you get.

JASON: Let the light hit it too.

INTERN BRANDON: There's red in there. There's red in there.

TRAVIS: There's red *in* there? Okay. That's one, then.

JASON: That means it's Red Beard then. I'm not shitting on you. I think it's awesome. Red Beard is a great name.

INTERN BRANDON: Red Beard is a good one. Red Beard is more pirate. That's a pirate name.

JASON: He's mad, which is cool.

JASON
HE'S MAD, WHICH IS COOL.

TRAVIS
I'M NOT MAD AT ALL.

TRAVIS: I'm not mad at all. There's nothing wrong with someone *having* a red beard. I'm saying you're throwing me into a boat that I'm not in. Like, there's people out here with actual red beards.

JASON: Well, yeah, there's redd*er* beards. I just think if you have any redness to your beard, you can be called Red Beard.

TRAVIS: No.

JASON: But red beards, I think are a little bit more lenient.

TRAVIS: No. This is why they're all dumb questions.

JASON: I'm just thinking of good beard nicknames. What's a good Nordic freaking—

TRAVIS: You can't look it up.

JASON: *[shouting at his phone]* Nordic for "Travis"!

TRAVIS: This is what I'm saying. You can't look it up. You have to just look at it, feel the energy.

JASON: *[typing into Google]* How do you say "Travis" in Norse?

TRAVIS: You did this, Brandon.

INTERN BRANDON: I know.

JASON: It might just be "Travis."

INTERN BRANDON: I fucked up. I can't leave open-ended questions in the show anymore.

JASON: Viking names.

TRAVIS: What?

INTERN BRANDON: What about Ragnar?

JASON: Duuude! Ragnar is great.

INTERN BRANDON: Did I get it? Did I nail it?

JASON: Similar to "Travis."

INTERN BRANDON: It's nowhere near "Travis."

[Jason Googles]

JASON: Translate the "Travis."

TRAVIS: God damn it, Jason.

[Jason Googles some more]

JASON: Celtic.

INTERN BRANDON: God damn it.

[Jason Googles some more]

TRAVIS: Jason's stuck. He's in a wormhole. He doesn't get out of these things. *[to Brandon]* You did this.

INTERN BRANDON: I know. Every week I do this and I reflect upon this. I'm like, "Never do that again."

[fast-forwarding again while Jason still Googles]

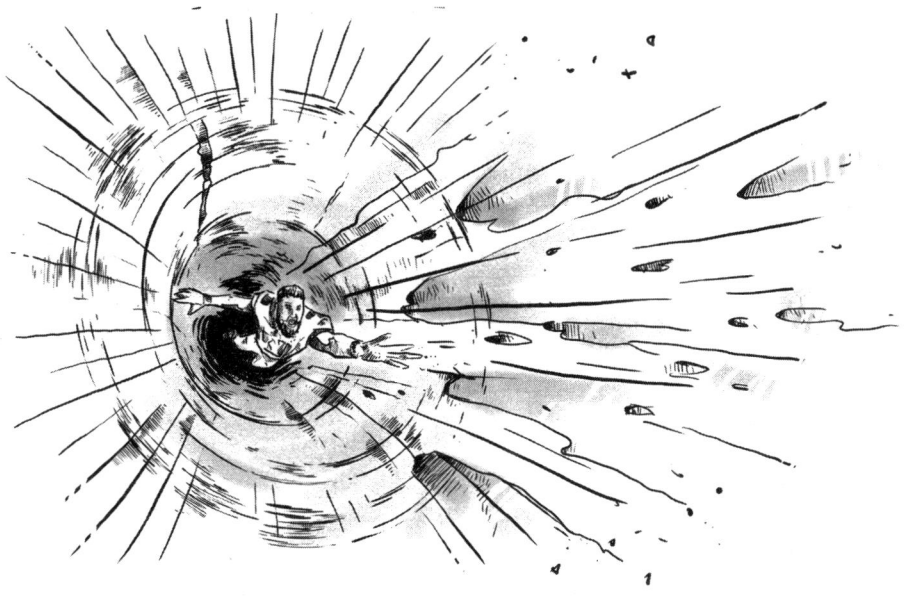

INTERN BRANDON: Tomislav, the first king of Croatia.

TRAVIS: Travislav?

INTERN BRANDON: Travislav! Travislav?

JASON: That's good. Travislav. I mean, it's Slavic.

INTERN BRANDON: Oh, fuck!

JASON: You got there, Travis.

INTERN BRANDON: Thank you.

JASON: Travislav.

INTERN BRANDON: Travislav!

If you could pick one article of clothing to wear for the rest of your life, what would it be?

92%er: @WhiTaysVersion via X

TRAVIS: That's a tough question. Where am I at in the world?

JASON: Does this mean if I pick a shirt, I can't wear pants?

TRAVIS: Again, there's not enough to this question.

JASON: Let's assume it's an outfit. Let's say you get shoes, a lower half, and upper half. That's what you get.

TRAVIS: Where am I at?

JASON: Well, this is the whole point. You don't know. It has to be ready to adapt to any place that you might be.

TRAVIS: Well, then I'll go hoodie and sweatpants and some Jordans.

JASON: Hoodie, sweatpants, and some Jordans.

TRAVIS: Actually, not Jordans. I got to go like combat boots.

JASON: I was about to say you can't go Jordans.

TRAVIS: You can't go Jordans. Combat boots. All-purpose.

JASON: And that's why they're combat boots. They got to be ready for everything.

TRAVIS: If it starts to get really hot, roll those fuckers up. Shorten those sleeves up. Maybe get rid of the hoodie. Put it in your fucking . . . pouch.

JASON: Are you allowed to take it off?

TRAVIS: That's what I'm saying. You just cut the hoodie, put it in your sweatshirt pouch, though.

JASON: Well, if you cut it, then it's ruined forever.

TRAVIS: No, then you put it in your pouch, and when you need it again, you just put it right on.

JASON: So it's a zippered hoodie. One of those zippered ones.

TRAVIS: Just tuck it underneath the . . . you can find a way.

JASON: I would go wool clothing because it's antimicrobial, so I don't have to worry about it getting as dirty as cotton or synthetic materials. A decent medium-thickness wool so that I'm pretty warm most of the time and I'm trying to stay out of cold climates. I would go with a decent medium-wool sweat because it's breathable so that when it's hot out, you still get some breathability and when it's cold out, it still retains some insulatory properties. And then I would go wool socks and I would go hiking boots so that you're kind of good to do whatever you want.

TRAVIS: You are going to be one smelly motherfucker because wool everything is going to be hot as fuck.

JASON: No, no, it breathes.

TRAVIS: No, it doesn't.

JASON: Wool is a known breathable.

TRAVIS: Jason.

JASON: Yeah?

TRAVIS: You wear wool in eighty-degree weather, you are sweating your ass off.

JASON: Well, just roll the pant legs up.

TRAVIS: The shit's on your back and your chest. If it's on your shoulders, you're going to start to sweat.

JASON: What did you say you were going for pants?

TRAVIS: Sweatpants.

JASON: You don't think that's going to be hot in eighty degrees?

TRAVIS: No. Not if I roll it up.

JASON: What are you talking about?

TRAVIS: Not if I roll it up.

JASON: But if you get the wool, the wool breathes better than cotton. Are you going cotton sweatpants?

TRAVIS: No.

JASON: What are you going?

TRAVIS: I'm going wool sweatpants.

JASON: You going synthetic sweatpants? Everyone knows it's wool sweatpants.

TRAVIS: You guys, come up with some really fucking good dumb questions—or, not-dumb questions.

10

Pop Culture

Will you guys lead the charge to finally move the Super Bowl to Saturday?

92%er: @Joedfran via X

TRAVIS: Lead the charge? No.

JASON: Yeah, I'm out on this.

TRAVIS: No, completely out. It's one day out of the year, all right? One day.

JASON: Football is meant to be played on Sunday. There are occasions where it's cool to see a Monday game. It's cool to see a Friday, a Saturday, a Thursday. But I think the Super Bowl is meant to be played on Sunday. If anything, we need to make Monday a holiday. The country should change what they're doing for the Super Bowl, not the Super Bowl for the country.

TRAVIS: Come on now, people.

JASON: Come on now.

TRAVIS: It's football, baby.

SUPER BOWL MONDAY SHOULD JUST BE OFF. UNLESS YOU WORK AT ANY OF THE STORES THAT I NEED TO GO TO, THEN YOU SHOULD STILL WORK.

JASON: I was in Brazil for the World Cup. Did you know, whenever the Brazilian national soccer team plays, the entire country shuts down? It's a national holiday whenever their soccer team plays.

TRAVIS: Yeah, what are we doing in America?

JASON: That's what I'm saying, just make it a national holiday. It's America's sport. It's surpassed our national pastime of baseball, in my opinion.

TRAVIS: I'm right there with you.

JASON: Super Bowl Monday should just be off. Unless you work at any of the stores that I need to go to, then you should still work.

TRAVIS: Unless you're Chick-fil-A, because you're off on Sunday.

JASON: Unless you're necessary. If you were open during COVID, you still got to go to work. It's how it works. Sorry, I don't make the rules.

TRAVIS: Rules are rules, America.

JASON: If you're necessary, you got to get out there.

Would you subject yourself to a roast? And if so, who would you want to roast you besides each other, of course?

92%er: @MandyAsberry via X

JASON: Let's say in this hypothetical world that we agreed to do something as ridiculous as a roast. Who would you want to roast you?

TRAVIS: Well, [Andrew] Santino is one of my favorite comedians of all time, and I think he would fucking deliver. Dave Chappelle is the all-time great. Kevin Hart, I would love Kevin to go up there and just fucking rip me in half. Yeah, basically all my favorite comedians.

JASON: If I was picking who to roast me, I would pick people that I would have no problem getting into a fistfight with, like family members. I'd let Dad roast me, but I'm going to beat the fuck out of Dad when the camera turns off.

TRAVIS: You just see me and Jason, I'm running from Jason like Tom and Jerry just like, "Fuck! It was a joke!"

JASON: We're just having fun.

TRAVIS: You got to have big Ed up there. Take a few strays. Am I saying that right? Strays. I don't know why that's my vocab for it.

JASON: No, it's good.

TRAVIS: Catch the strays!

JASON: I get when it's your friends and close people, but when it's random celebrities up there . . . the one person I wouldn't allow on the stage is Kylie. She has way too much. I can't.

TRAVIS: She knows too much.

JASON: I can't, yeah. Princess Kiana. I can't allow that.

TRAVIS: Princess Kiana is going to go up there and fucking torch you.

JASON: I mean, every day I'm getting roasted by Kylie. I don't need her to go up onstage and do that.

TRAVIS: And that's what I'm saying. It's almost like an honor to get—

JASON: Shit on?

TRAVIS: Yeah, just shit on. But if you're open to it, go online. You can get fucking roasted. Like a lot of these jokes have already been said.

JASON: I'm already getting roasted, I guess.

TRAVIS: Just look in the comments. That'll humble you.

11

G.O.A.T.s

If you had to rank your favorite cereals, what would your top five be?

TRAVIS: It's hard to just name five.

JASON: This is a good question because I've recently gotten back into the cereal game. I probably didn't—before I had kids—I probably didn't have cereal for a long time. It was completely removed from my diet.

TRAVIS: I never got away from cereal. I've always been going and getting some good two percent milk.

JASON: Two percent? I'm a whole milk guy now. We grew up on two percent, but I'm all about that whole milk.

TRAVIS: There's something about the childhood nostalgia of going up there and just getting that blue top.

JASON: The blue top? Yeah, I hear you. Yeah, let's start at five. What are you going with?

TRAVIS: Fifth-ranked? Man, fifth can't be a fan favorite. It's kind of got to be for me just a consistent, always good for me. That's Apple Jacks, man. I fucking love some good Apple Jacks, man.

JASON: Great cereal. It is very good, man. I was thinking the same lines that you were thinking, but I was even going more basic. And that's Cheerios.

TRAVIS: Cheerios are higher up there though.

JASON: You can get to the rest of yours. Let me do my number five, okay? I'm going Cheerios because of the ability to dress them up. You can do whatever you want to them.

TRAVIS: That's why they're higher on the list.

JASON: Well, we'll see what the fans think. I got them at five because as a stand-alone, Cheerios aren't bringing much to the table compared to some of the other higher items. But from where they're at, I don't care if it's Honey Nut. I don't even know if they make regular Cheerios anymore. I've only ever had it. But you can put sugar on it. You can put fruit in there. We used to have so much.

TRAVIS: We used to have the freaking pot of fucking sugar.

JASON: I know exactly what you're talking about. But that's why they're five. Because you have to add sugar to it. They're trying to be a little bit too healthy.

TRAVIS: They snuck in Frosted Cheerios and fucking completely changed the game.

JASON: But those aren't as good. It's not as good as the dumping your own sugar on it. There's part of that process of dressing the Cheerios up.

TRAVIS: But then you dump the sugar on the Frosted Cheerios. And add strawberries and oh my gosh, that's how you wake up in the morning, kids.

JASON: What's your four? What's your four spot?

TRAVIS: Damn, this is where it gets tight. It's where it gets tough, man. I have to go Cap'n [Crunch's] Crunch Berries.

JASON: If I was a child, I would have said the same thing, but I've gotten off of Cap'n Crunch Berries as an adult. But it's very good cereal.

TRAVIS: Dude, so good.

JASON: I wrote mine down because I have my notepad that you made fun of me for, so I have my list already made up. I have just regular Cap'n Crunch at number four. I didn't know if I wanted to put Cap'n Crunch Berries or Peanut Butter Cap'n Crunch in this same spot. I like all three.

TRAVIS: Oh, Peanut Butter Cap'n Crunch is so fucking good.

JASON: I just went with the original.

TRAVIS: That's fair.

JASON: I'm putting them all at number four. I still prefer on like a standard, regular basis old-school Cap'n Crunch, even though it does cut the shit out of the roof of your mouth. It's delicious. What do you got, three?

TRAVIS: I'm going to say you can have Cheerios in your top five. I don't want them in there, aka I fucked up my order and now I'm just going to leave them off. I'm going Lucky Charms. You can't beat the marshmallows.

JASON: I think it's good. It's a good pick. Very solid pick.

TRAVIS: It's hard for me to keep it at three, but you can't beat these next two.

JASON: I think we're going to have some similar ones in the top three, but we'll find out.

TRAVIS: Well, we grew up in the same house.

JASON: Number three, I got Cinnamon Toast Crunch. Love Cinnamon Toast Crunch.

TRAVIS: It's got to be on the top five.

JASON: You don't think it's in the top five?

TRAVIS: No, it's got to be. That's probably my number two.

JASON: Yeah, that's like the best go-to. We're just putting milk in this thing and it's going to be effin' delicious.

TRAVIS: Effin' delicious, yeah.

JASON: Yeah, fuckin' delicious. And as to your Lucky Charms at number three, I have Lucky Charms at number two.

TRAVIS: So we just flopped, we flopped Cap'n Crunch and Lucky Charms.

JASON: I guess so, yeah. So, where are you at? What's your number two?

TRAVIS: Cap'n Crunch.

JASON: Cap'n Crunch, nice.

TRAVIS: No, no, no, no, no, no, no, no, no, no, no, no, no, no, no, no. Cinnamon Toast Crunch.

TRAVIS
NO, NO, NO, NO, NO, NO, NO, NO, NO, NO, NO, NO, NO, NO, NO. CINNAMON TOAST CRUNCH.

JASON: That's fine. So, two and three for both of us is Lucky Charms, Cinnamon Toast Crunch. Number one, should we say it at the same time? If it's gonna be the same one?

TRAVIS: It's one thousand percent the same one. Three, two, one.

[simultaneously]

TRAVIS: Reese's Puffs.

JASON: Reese's Peanut Butter Puffs.

JASON: Yeeeeeeeeeeah!

TRAVIS: Dude, it's undefeated, dude.

JASON: It's so freaking good. It's candy.

TRAVIS: It's the best.

JASON: It's just candy in cereal form.

TRAVIS: I could eat a whole box right now, literally an entire box. I could fucking put it in a popcorn bowl and just fucking add the entire gallon of milk to it and just walk it. Just absolutely walk it. I will eat it. It will take me like three hours to do it and I'll just be eating the soggy ones at the bottom that I still enjoy because the cereal is so fucking good.

JASON: Dude, I'm not a big fan of Reese's Puffs dry. I like it medium soggy to completely soggy.

TRAVIS: Yep.

JASON: Like I think it's better when the milk starts getting into that. I think it's ridiculous that it's a cereal that you give children to eat. "Dad, can I have candy for breakfast?" "No, don't be ridiculous. You got to eat something that's good for you. Have some Reese's Peanut Butter Puffs."

TRAVIS: Dude . . .

JASON: I don't really see that that's much different.

TRAVIS: We used to have boxes of that shit, dude, boxes.

JASON: Well, that's because it was delicious. And I think Dad folded because he loves Reese's.

TRAVIS: And he used to sneak a bowl in when we left.

JASON: He really didn't like us eating Lucky Charms. But for some reason, Reese's Peanut Butter Puffs, he didn't care about.

TRAVIS: Peanut butter. It's got protein in it.

Who are the top three movie villains of all time?

92%er: @FakeMannyJ via X

TRAVIS: We could go any direction. We talking horror films? We talking action movies? We talking comedies? What are we talking? I think all my villains are going to be based off comedy and action movies because I'm not really a big horror-film kind of guy.

JASON: Sure. It's too easy, too. It's too obvious. Freddy Krueger?

TRAVIS: Yeah, no shit. *Texas Chainsaw Massacre*?

JASON: Cool.

TRAVIS: I hope they don't come after me. Do we go top three?

JASON: Top three. Okay. My number one, my number one. I'll go for . . .

TRAVIS: Joker.

JASON: Joker?!

TRAVIS: I'm going. Joker is definitely top three.

JASON: You're fucking throwing a superhero villain at . . . come on, dude.

TRAVIS: What do you mean? It's an unbelievable role.

JASON: If you wear makeup, you can't be considered a great villain.

TRAVIS: I can't wait to hear your villain. Go ahead. Who are you going with? We'll go back.

JASON: Ernie McCracken [Bill Murray in *Kingpin*].

TRAVIS: Ernie McCracken . . . that's a good villain. Yeah, it's a good villain. I think he's got some of the best lines you could ever think of.

JASON: He's got cleverness. He's got deception. Mischief. Talent. He's got it all. And he's got the look. He's got the look . . .

TRAVIS: Especially when that hair gets going frizzy and like kind of at the end of a bowling match, like he really looks like he's the villain. Who am I going with next? Since you're going comedy, I'll go comedy. I'm going White Goodman, Globo Gym, Ben Stiller.

JASON: Ben Stiller. Nice. I actually think that's not Ben Stiller's best villain. His best villain is in *Heavyweights* as . . .

TRAVIS: The same character! It's just with kids.

JASON: It's better though. The lines are better.

TRAVIS: No, it is not.

JASON: "How you doing, little Tony?" "Bad."

TRAVIS: The whole movie is iconic. There's only one of those movies out here.

JASON: I love *Dodgeball*. I think maybe it's just the nostalgia of *Heavyweights*. I think that's a better Ben Stiller villain. Either way, Ben Stiller as a villain. I think we should just take Ben Stiller as a villain.

TRAVIS: I'll just take Ben Stiller.

JASON: You take him in both of those. You can take him in *Happy Gilmore* as the evil nanny sitter.

TRAVIS: Oh my gosh. This dude is one of the most iconic villains of all time.

JASON: Good take, good take. I'll go Willy Wonka.

TRAVIS: I must be missing something.

JASON: What are you missing? He killed a bunch of kids in his chocolate factory, Travis.

TRAVIS: Jason, he did not kill a single one.

JASON: Not only that, but he had—

TRAVIS: They're all—

JASON: Not only that, but he kidnapped a bunch of Oompa-Loompas and has

JASON
I'LL GO WILLY WONKA.

TRAVIS
I MUST BE MISSING SOMETHING.

JASON
WHAT ARE YOU MISSING? HE KILLED A BUNCH OF KIDS IN HIS CHOCOLATE FACTORY, TRAVIS.

them working in his fucking chocolate factory. He's one of the most notorious.

TRAVIS: You see the way those Oompa-Loompas dance and have fun in that place? They fucking love that place. They definitely signed up.

JASON: Come on now. They don't have a choice.

TRAVIS: They don't have a choice?

JASON: They don't have a choice.

TRAVIS: Yeah, because the kids need candy.

JASON: No, because nobody's allowed to leave the chocolate factory.

TRAVIS: So Santa's holding a whole bunch of elves hostage up in the North Pole.

JASON: There's no rule that if the elves leave—

TRAVIS: You're calling Santa a villain?

JASON: No, there's a clear rule in the Willy Wonka the Chocolate Movie that you can't leave the factory. I mean, it's explicit.

TRAVIS: Yeah.

JASON: That's not an explicit rule of Santa.

TRAVIS: Either way . . .

JASON: Santa's employing a bunch of elves that wouldn't have jobs otherwise. He's just providing labor. And paying for it with sugar.

TRAVIS: Who was my last villain? Who did I have as my last villain? Oh, one of my favorites of all time, Dr. Evil.

JASON: Oh, dude, that's a good one.

TRAVIS: Dr. Evil is a legendary villain.

JASON: He's even got a miniature version of himself.

TRAVIS: I love those Austin Powers movies.

JASON: Those are electric.

TRAVIS: Dude, they were so much fun. I watched one the other day, the one with Beyoncé. Damn, which one was that? Was that one?

JASON: Beyoncé was two, I think.

TRAVIS: Yeah, *Goldmember.*

JASON: Yeah, that's it.

TRAVIS: Number three. That was number three. Wow. Damn, there were some good ones before. This might be the best trilogy of all time.

JASON: *Goldmember* was with Fat Bastard. I do remember that.

TRAVIS: Damn, that was a good one, too.

JASON: So I still have one more left.

TRAVIS: Yeah, you got one more.

JASON: I mean, I got to go Ivan Drago. "If he dies, he dies."

TRAVIS: That's lame.

JASON: Why is that lame?

TRAVIS: It's not a good villain.

JASON: He killed Apollo Creed. Do you have no fucking heart?

TRAVIS: *[long sigh]* No. Not for Drago.

JASON: Well, you would have heart for Apollo. He's the one that died. I think we need another *Rocky* movie because I mean . . . it united everybody. It united everybody and ended the Cold War. And I think we need more movies like that. "If you could change, we could change. All of us could change." What is it? "If I could change, you could change . . . We all can change." Ah, whatever . . .

TRAVIS: You need to *change* your villain is what you need to do because that last one was pretty buns.

JASON: Hey, you're over here naming the Joker. Real original.

TRAVIS: Heath Ledger won awards for that.

JASON: He did. Heath did a great job. Heath made a terrible superhero movie somehow spectacular.

TRAVIS: It's the legendary villain, see?

What is the best Girl Scout cookie?

92%er: GSmama208 via Club 92

JASON: Please, when I say this, do not send me a bunch of boxes of these Girl Scout cookies.

TRAVIS: Don't you do it. Don't you do it.

JASON: Like our favorite cereal and our favorite candy, it's something with peanut butter and chocolate because that's the best combination in the world. Tagalongs.

TRAVIS: Tagalongs.

JASON: Hands down. I've noticed this, depending on what area you're at in the country, there's different Girl Scout cookies and brands and they're not always named the same.

TRAVIS: I've only seen one. It's that red box.

JASON: They're both red, but I feel like in one part of the country, they're called Tagalongs and another part of the country, they might be called something else. Let's look this up.

TRAVIS: What other good ones are there? There's just a straight-up sugar cookie. I think that's the blue box.

JASON: Yep.

TRAVIS: That one's pretty good. Ooh, the lemon cookies I do enjoy though. They're a nice switch-up.

JASON: Lemon cookie? There's a lemon cookie?

TRAVIS: Yeah. It's like the yellow one. I'm pretty sure.

JASON: The yellow one's like Samoa, I thought, or is that purple?

TRAVIS: Purple is the coconut. Those are good. The oatmeal coconut. Those're dangerous too.

JASON: Anyways, we answered the question.

TRAVIS: It's . . . Tagalongs. You can't beat it. They're everyone's favorite.

What are the top five movies of all time that are set in Las Vegas?

92%er: @AustinTxChief via X

TRAVIS: That's damn good. That's a damn good question right there.

JASON: I think we both are going to say the first one. I'll let you say it. I know where you're going.

TRAVIS: Three, two, one.

[simultaneously]

TRAVIS

THREE, TWO, ONE.
(SIMULTANEOUSLY)

TRAVIS

HANGOVER.

JASON

VEGAS VACATION.

TRAVIS: *Hangover.*

JASON: *Vegas Vacation.*

JASON: Oh my gosh.

TRAVIS: I do love *Vegas Vacation.*

JASON: You said you love *Vegas Vacation.* I thought that's where you were going. *Hangover*'s great. They're both good movies. They're both so good.

TRAVIS: I was so disappointed when I went to Vegas for the first time and there was no like . . .

JASON: Free cars to win?

TRAVIS: Free cars to win. I was just like, where the fuck do I get a free Hummer?

JASON: Where are all these free cars? Randy is the uncle. What's the son's name? I can't remember those. Rusty. I knew it was an *R*. Randy Quaid is the best part of those movies. Chevy Chase is great, too, but God damn, Randy's good. Yeah. *Vegas Vacation, Hangover.* Those are both of my top five. Are you a big *Swingers* guy?

TRAVIS: "Vegas, baby, Vegas."

JASON: I'm just a big Vince Vaughn fan.

TRAVIS: "You're so money you don't even know it."

JASON: Dude, Vince Vaughn is just an electric freaking character.

TRAVIS: He's a legend.

JASON: Him and Jon Favreau, they are the absolute legends. They were in *Four Christmases* together.

JASON: *Four Christmases.* The best romcom of all time, *The Break-Up*, which I don't think Jon Favreau is in, but Vince Vaughn is electric in that one. Anyways, *Swingers* outstanding movie.

TRAVIS: What about would you consider *Rush Hour*? Was that in Vegas?

JASON: Is that in Vegas?

TRAVIS: They have a casino in LA?

JASON: At the time, they probably didn't. I would bet it would have been illegal to have a casino at the time. You got to put *Casino* in there. [Martin] Scorsese.

TRAVIS: It's a classic. You could throw it on right now, I'd watch it.

JASON: [Robert] De Niro. *Casino, Goodfellas, Bronx Tale.* I mean, you can't go wrong with anything in that category.

TRAVIS: Are you sure *Rush Hour* wasn't in Vegas?

JASON: No, I'm not. I literally just was told this by Intern Brandon.

TRAVIS: You sure?

JASON: I'm not sure. Maybe it's *Rush Hour 2*. *Rush Hour 2* is the one where they're in the casino, right? You know, where he jumps down the banner. That's *Rush Hour 2*. That's not *Rush Hour 1*.

TRAVIS: All right.

JASON: Check *Rush Hour 2*. Is that in Vegas?

TRAVIS: It's in a casino.

INTERN BRANDON: Here's the plot line for *Rush Hour 2*. "It's vacation time for Detective James Kyrie. Find yourself alongside Detective Lee in Hong Kong . . ."

TRAVIS: Hong Kong.

JASON: Well, they end up in Vegas, though.

TRAVIS: Hong Kong, the Vegas of Japan.

JASON: I'll allow that. Technically, it was a British territory, I think, at the time. All right. One more movie.

TRAVIS: Vegas is a British territory?

JASON: *[hangs head in disappointment]*

TRAVIS: I ain't buying it. We're missing one. It's right there.

JASON: OK, so we got *Vegas Vacation, Hangover, Swingers, Casino*. And I thought you already said *Ocean's 11*.

TRAVIS: Yeah, but there's one . . .

JASON: There's one other one that we're missing.

TRAVIS: Which one is it?

JASON: *Big Trouble in Little Chinatown* [*sic*]. Oh, is that the name of that movie?

TRAVIS: *Dodgeball.*

JASON: Does that take place in Vegas?

TRAVIS: I knew there was one.

JASON: That's definitely up there.

[they do a shitty high five]

JASON: I think we got to get a better one than that for *Dodgeball.*

[they high-five slightly better]

TRAVIS: Well, fucking extend your arm.

JASON: It's my left hand, I don't—

TRAVIS: Watch the elbow. Dude, well, that's our top five. And yes, we just made *Dodgeball* a Vegas movie.

JASON: It's official. It's Vegas.

12

Cuisine

Do you put the cereal first or the milk first?

92%er: @AelinHerondale4 via X

JASON: Do I put the cereal first or the milk first?

TRAVIS: And this is why we have this fucking segment in here as "No Dumb Questions." This is about as stupid of a question as I've ever heard. Everyone knows the cereal goes in first.

JASON: Be careful, Trav. Be careful what you say.

TRAVIS: *Everyone* knows the cereal goes in first.

JASON: I don't know if you're aware—

TRAVIS: You have to lather up all the cereal.

JASON: Travis, I'm on the same page with you.

TRAVIS: You don't just pour it in one part of the bowl either. You pour it over the top and you get everything covered in milk.

JASON: I'm one hundred percent with you. There's no logical reason to pour the cereal second. But for some reason, Kylie pours the cereal second.

TRAVIS: *What?!*

JASON: And it's never made sense to me. I don't know why. I mean, in no other situation where a solid goes into a liquid would you ever put the solid in second. Like, it's just asking for a disaster to happen.

TRAVIS: Yeah, it doesn't make any sense.

JASON: You don't fill a glass up to the brim and then start loading ice cubes in that motherfucker. You're going to get water all over the place. What are we doing here?

TRAVIS: Yeah.

JASON

YOU DON'T FILL A GLASS UP TO THE BRIM AND THEN START LOADING ICE CUBES IN THAT MOTHERFUCKER. YOU'RE GOING TO GET WATER ALL OVER THE PLACE.

JASON: But Kylie does do it that way.

TRAVIS: That doesn't make any sense.

JASON: And I usually don't say anything because it's none of my business, even though I think it's ridiculous.

TRAVIS: It's not the argument to start.

JASON: And also it doesn't make it taste better. Like, if you just like dry cereal, what are you putting the milk anywhere with it? Like, there's a reason you put the milk in second because it gets the cereal to the perfect consistency of moisture.

TRAVIS: Dude, it's . . . thank you.

JASON: So, Ky, you're wrong on this one. I'm pretty sure if we put a poll out, you'd be in the bottom eight percent of the ninety-two percent.

TRAVIS: Well, there's only one way to find out. Ninety-two percenters, we will have a poll. So, let us know who's in the right here.

New Heights ✓
@newheightshow

What say you, 92%ers?

| Cereal before milk | 93.4% |
| Milk before cereal | 6.6% |

14,237 votes · Final results

What was your favorite "struggle meal" when you were broke? And what's the fanciest or most expensive thing you've ever eaten?

92%er: @humcupcake via X

JASON: So I'm devising from context what "struggle meal" means. Is this just like the politically correct way to say "broke-ass meal" or something like that? Like we'd call it struggle meal. I've never heard—

TRAVIS: I've never heard "struggle meal" either. But I understand.

JASON: I don't know why I don't like it. I don't like it.

TRAVIS: You're struggling.

JASON: What is your favorite, like, cheap-ass meal?

TRAVIS: I got a few good ones. The old Wendy's dollar menu. Fuck, yeah. No, you know, one of my fucking favorite things to do was in college after I went through my entire FAFSA check and my scholarship check would be to call Dad to tell him to call Domino's and put in a large pizza for me.

JASON: So your struggle was calling your parents.

TRAVIS: Yeah. I mean, I've had a beautiful life.

JASON: It works. I guess in college we've—you know, like, ramen noodles.

TRAVIS: I couldn't do ramen noodles, man.

JASON: Oh, I love ramen noodles. When I think of food, like . . . we don't have any money or we're like getting the bare bottom of the pantry. I think of ramen noodles. I think of beans and weenies. Big beans-and-weenies fan. That's one of my favorites.

TRAVIS: Hated beans and weenies.

JASON: Hamburger Helper. Does that count? Is that kind of like . . . ?

TRAVIS: Okay, TV dinners, yeah.

JASON: Just like heat-them-up-type deals.

TRAVIS: But that's the thing. Like if I'm struggling and I'm broke, I'm probably going to go to McDonald's and just get a few, like, things off of the dollar—

JASON: Off the value menu?

TRAVIS: I don't know if you can even do that anymore.

JASON: I don't think they're a dollar anymore. I think they've upped them.

TRAVIS: That's fucked.

JASON: What is your favorite value meal item at any fast-food chain?

TRAVIS: Dude, Junior Bacon Cheeseburger.

JASON: I mean, it's good. I feel like I had so many of them in college.

TRAVIS: You used to be able to get fucking nuggets for a dollar.

JASON: I know. I think I used to like them so much in college, I just kind of got turned off of JBCs. It's not as good to me anymore.

TRAVIS: You could always go and get Guy's Pizza, a slice for a dollar.

JASON: I mean, dude, if you're really cramped, you go in with a couple buddies for a Crave Case from White Castle.

TRAVIS: Ooh, White Castle, man. You're fucking *stuffed*.

JASON: Dude, that's a lot of sliders.

TRAVIS: I think it's like twenty.

JASON: I feel like Taco Bell didn't really have a great value menu. I think the whole menu is just kind of value.

TRAVIS: Dude, what? You could order the entire menu twice with like fucking $20. What?

JASON: I think that's what I'm saying. I think the whole thing was just value.

TRAVIS: You walk into fucking Taco Bell with $5, you can get fucking breakfast, lunch, and dinner.

JASON: I mean, before Subway started price gouging, those $5 footlongs, that's a pretty damn good deal.

TRAVIS: It is.

JASON: Yeah, as you can see, we've lived a life fully of privilege.

TRAVIS: I guess, yeah, cereal. Cereal is another one of them. You get a box for fucking a dollar and some change, you get a fuck ton of meals out of that box.

JASON: You ever ate cereal with water? I've done it.

TRAVIS: I mean—

JASON: It's not ideal.

TRAVIS: I'm not upset with just the crunch and not getting them soggy.

JASON: I like the sogginess, especially specific types of cereal. It's just better being a little soggy.

TRAVIS: You're like a soggy oatmeal guy too. I like mine a little bit more dry.

JASON: You like dry oatmeal?

TRAVIS: I like *drier* than soggy.

JASON: I don't like soup oatmeal, but I like there to be a consistency.

TRAVIS: Yeah, see, I can't do the soupy stuff. It's hard for me to do soupy stuff.

JASON: Do you like soup? What's your favorite soup?

TRAVIS: Like chicken noodle?

JASON: Soup is the original struggle meal.

TRAVIS: Chicken noodle, only at Campbell's Chicken Noodle? What are we talking about?

JASON: Really, any of the Campbell's soups, they qualify, right?

TRAVIS: I've only enjoyed chicken noodle. I only like that brothy soup. I don't like the fucking—

JASON: You don't like clam chowder?

TRAVIS: Yeah, the gloppy fucking thick shit. I'm out on that. The only thick-type soup I could do is like a bisque.

JASON: Yeah, I mean, this is the best we can do for you. I've heard of guys eating like ketchup sandwiches and mayonnaise sandwiches and—

TRAVIS: Sugar sandwich. That was my guy Reggie's go-to.

JASON

SUGAR SANDWICH? IS THAT WHAT I THINK IT IS?

TRAVIS

YEP.

JASON: Sugar sandwich? Is that what I think it is?

TRAVIS: Yep.

JASON: Yeah, it's exactly it?

TRAVIS: Yep.

JASON: That doesn't sound exciting one bit.

TRAVIS: I'm not gonna lie, I kind of fucked with it.

JASON: I mean, it's essentially what I used to do with a bagel and cinnamon sugar.

TRAVIS: Another one, bagel is another one.

All right, so let's transition this to the most expensive thing you've ever eaten.

JASON: There's a hundred-dollar cheesesteak at this restaurant, Barclay Prime, downtown Philadelphia.

TRAVIS: You pulled the trigger on it?

JASON: Well, I mean, we do a lot of O-line dinners there and stuff like that, where you're splurging as a group. And I have had that. I don't think it's the fanciest or most expensive thing, but there's something about it being a cheesesteak being that ridiculously priced that is, and it's very good. But I guess I'll vote that. I don't know. What do you got?

TRAVIS: Nice. I got nothing. I don't know. I don't necessarily look at the most expensive thing. And yeah, fancy foods are kind of just like, I love getting fucking big obnoxious steaks. So if I see like a porterhouse that's a forty-eight-ounce? I'm like, yea-ah, give me that! Medium! You cut it off the bone a little bit too.

JASON: Most of the higher-priced items are usually meat that has some type of alteration like, hey, you want this dry-aged fifty-two-ounce Tomahawk steak that's from Wagyu and it's like $300. I'm like, no, I want the regular rib eye that tastes fucking delicious without putting all that fungus on it. I don't need the fucking aging process.

TRAVIS: Give me the aging.

JASON: No, give me the regular steak, not Wagyu.

TRAVIS: Give me the Wagyu.

JASON: Give me the regular. I like a steak that tastes like a steak. I don't like a steak that tastes like it's been marinated in butter and then melts all over the place.

TRAVIS: It hasn't been marinated in butter.

JASON: All right, whatever. The fancy stuff nine times out of ten tastes worse. Just being honest with you. Unless, the one caveat to this, fancy pasta. You go to a nice Italian restaurant that's like upscale? Those pastas that come out—

TRAVIS: They're making that fucking pasta in the back.

Do either of you guys like pumpkin spice lattes or pumpkin-flavored anything, especially those little pumpkin cakes and cookies in grocery stores?

92%er: @msmlmorgan via X

JASON: Don't know. Never had one. Travis, what do you think about pumpkin spice lattes?

TRAVIS: Don't know. Never had one. Also, I really only do pumpkin seeds in my oatmeal in the mornings.

JASON: You do pumpkin seeds? Pumpkin seeds are pretty good. I'll agree with that. Are you a big pumpkin pie guy?

TRAVIS: I'm not a pie guy. I'm not a pie guy at all.

JASON: Yeah, but I feel like pumpkin pie is a little bit different. It's got a different texture than normal pie.

TRAVIS: Pie is pie.

JASON: Pie is pie? Not a pie guy? I got to get you down the shore, have a little Steve & Cookie's blueberry pie. I'm not a big pie guy, either, but that blueberry pie at Steve & Cookie's? Woo, it's pretty good.

I don't mind pumpkin pie in the right environment. It's a little cold outside. I see some leaves changing. For some reason, I get the itch to have some. But in general, I think pumpkin is an overrated flavor. I think it's similar to a lot of these advertising trends that people will do to try and get you to commerce their businesses, or making up national holidays. Like it means a damn thing—just to get you to buy whatever product that holiday is selling.

So in general, I do not fall victim to the pumpkin spice lattes, pumpkin cookies, pumpkin cakes. About the only thing I fall victim to is buying some of those cute little pumpkins to put on my front porch. And I do look forward to making some jack-o'-lanterns this year with the girls. That will be a fun project.

TRAVIS: Make sure you share. Can't wait to see that as well. I'm right there with you. I'm not a big pumpkin anything other than pumpkin seeds in my granola. That's just 'cause they're beneficial.

JASON: I will do *Reese's* pumpkin, the Reese's Halloween edition that are shaped like little pumpkins.

TRAVIS: I haven't had those in forever.

JASON: I've fallen victim to those ones. But really, I'm just looking for an excuse to buy Reese's at that point.

TRAVIS: I'm in on seasonal stuff, though.

JASON: What seasonal stuff are you in on?

TRAVIS: I like a fall harvest. Yeah, I'm like a fall harvest, like Cup of Joe.

JASON: What's a fall harvest Cup of Joe? I think you just told me you like pumpkin spice lattes, is what you just told me. You're describing a pumpkin spice latte.

TRAVIS: It's not pumpkin though.

JASON: It is.

TRAVIS: It's just like a cinnamon spice.

JASON: Bro . . . pumpkin spice lattes have cinnamon and pumpkin.

TRAVIS: Yeah, but not pumpkin. What I'm talking about isn't pumpkin.

JASON: So you're talking about more of like, it's later fall, around the holidays of like post-Thanksgiving, maybe. Like what they put on the rim almost for a Christmas ale. I'll do that. I fall victim to some Christmas ale.

TRAVIS: Christmas ale.

JASON: Gosh. Great Lakes gets me on that.

TRAVIS: I am in on coffee being seasonal. I think sometimes it just matches the air. It just connects perfectly.

JASON: Should I try my first pumpkin spice latte?

TRAVIS: Yeah. Give us a good Jason Kelce review. Shoot on down to Dunkin' Donuts or—

JASON: Looks like I'm going to Starbucks tomorrow.

TRAVIS: Starbucks, yeah. And get your first pumpkin spice latte. Let us know what you think.

When making a peanut butter and jelly sandwich, do you put them on separate pieces or spread them together?

92%er: @jdubs8397 via YouTube

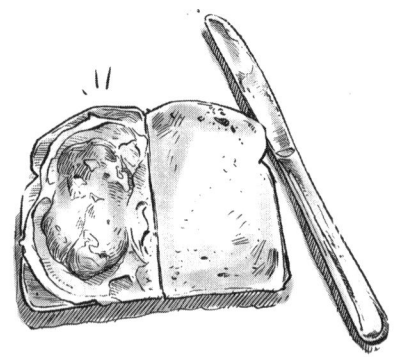

TRAVIS: I am not a psychopath. I put the jelly on one side and the peanut butter on the other side and then put them together. Nobody in their right fucking mind spreads peanut butter and jelly on one slice and then puts a . . . that's just not how it's done.

JASON: Is that real?

TRAVIS: Nobody fucking does that.

JASON: Is that real?

TRAVIS

NOBODY DOES THAT. THERE'S NO WAY ANYBODY DOES THAT.

TRAVIS: Nobody does that. There's no way anybody does that.

JASON: Why would you put the jelly on the peanut . . . ? Do you put . . . so do you put the peanut butter on the jelly? You'd have to go jelly on peanut butter, right?

TRAVIS: No, yeah, you have to do a layer of peanut butter and then the jelly. *If* you were to do that, but that doesn't make any sense.

JASON: Yeah, why would you? I don't understand.

TRAVIS: You wouldn't get a smooth, easy spread. You would be making your job harder.

JASON: It feels like there's more control and it's easier to determine how much is going on if it's done on different pieces of bread. Yeah, there's something that sounds really off about putting the peanut butter and the jelly on the same side. I mean, I guess that's how I build a sandwich. If I'm building ham, lettuce, tomato, cheese, all of that would be piled on top of the same thing. But then I put the mayonnaise on the bread.

TRAVIS: But you have to spread, yeah. Whatever you have to spread, it has to go on, like a—

JASON: A piece of bread.

TRAVIS: Yeah, an even surface, yeah.

JASON: I think that's right, because it's just easier to spread it. You're not, like, contaminating the layers.

TRAVIS: You're not fucking up your masterpiece. I hate a sloppy sandwich, man. I like my shit nice and fucking perfect.

JASON: I like a nice little sloppy cheesesteak. You get cheese all over your face. God, that's good.

TRAVIS: You like that shit with Whiz.

JASON: I like it with American, but I will eat it with Whiz. It's actually not bad if you try it.

TRAVIS: Nacho cheese and bread is ridiculous.

JASON: I'm not a big Cheez Whiz person, but Whiz on a cheesesteak isn't bad. I've had it before. Definitely prefer American. Dude, this is another thing. I want to figure out how to make the best burger. There's something about cheeseburgers that I just love.

TRAVIS: Come on over, I'll teach you.

JASON: I want Andy to teach me, that's who I want to teach me. I want Andy Reid to show me the spread. He's got to know the best cheeseburger he's ever had.

Yeah, I'm with you. Any type of spread goes right on top of the bread.

TRAVIS: On the bread only. Anytime you got to spread something, you put it on the bread. If you're going to spread, put it on the bread.

JASON: There we go. It's a simple rule. And easy to follow.

NEW DUMB QUESTION

Name your top five places/ situations to drink a beer.

92%er: that_hurts via X

TRAVIS: Number one: anywhere. Are you kidding me?

JASON: Beat me to it. Number one was anywhere that serves a beer. Any place you can buy a beer is number one. Number two: anywhere near water, right? On a beach, lake, ocean, stream, puddle, doesn't really matter.

TRAVIS: Pool. Creek.

JASON: Water sewage treatment facility. Anything works near fluids.

TRAVIS: Number three: anywhere there's a sporting activity—any type of competition.

JASON: Boom. So good.

TRAVIS: Any type of sports competition. I'm in on having a beer, watching some competition go down.

JASON: Any type of family event or friendly get-together. Could be a barbecue, could be a holiday, could be a funeral.

TRAVIS: A funeral could be . . . you kidding me? You think?

JASON: I gotta say this: your fucking garage. Few places better than to freaking enjoy a nice cold beer after a hard day's work of chores.

TRAVIS: Yeah, or just in your home, at the end of the day. Emphasize *end of the day*.

PART 4

CRAZY
SH*T

13

Mindbenders

How many holes does a straw have?

92%er: @LukeBottar via X

TRAVIS: It's just one hole, man.

JASON: We can't do like the standard "Is a hot dog a sandwich?" Is a straw—how many holes in the straw? We're looking for a little bit more innovation than this. I mean, clearly straws have two holes that are connected in the middle.

TRAVIS: Shut the fuck up, you're ridiculous. You don't even believe that, you don't even believe it.

JASON: What? It's two holes.

TRAVIS: It's one hole.

JASON: What makes it one hole? That it's connected? So it's one hole?

TRAVIS: No, it's just one hole. There's not—

JASON: It goes all the way through.

TRAVIS: Just because it has a start and a finish doesn't mean it has two holes. It's one hole.

JASON: So, if you have a hole that's open and it's going straight and then it curves to the left, and then you have a hole that continues—

TRAVIS: You're changing the question.

JASON: I'm just asking! What is your definition of a hole?

TRAVIS: A definition of a hole is that there's a start and a finish to the hole. There's nothing breaking it or stopping it. So, if it's just . . . if there could be multiple ends to the hole, but it is one hole.

JASON: So, if you have a straw that's continuous, and then it has four other shooting points to come off of it, that's all just one hole? Like a groundhog, like an ant hole is just a big old . . . it's just one hole.

TRAVIS: One hole.

JASON: Yeah, I think that's preposterous. It's ridiculous. I think—

TRAVIS: I think a straw has one hole.

JASON: This is the thing. This is the thing!

TRAVIS: I think an ant farm is something completely different.

JASON: This is why I hate these types of questions.

TRAVIS: But you changed the entire question!

JASON: I'm going to explain to you—

TRAVIS: Why is a straw two holes?

JASON: If you would allow me to talk, I'll explain.

TRAVIS: Why is it . . . explain yourself!

JASON: This is my problem with these questions. The only reasons they exist is for people to come up with arbitrary definitions.

Is a hot dog a sandwich? Would you ever call a fucking hot dog a sandwich?

TRAVIS: No.

JASON: I don't give a fuck whether, "Oh, it's in between two slices of bread." Okay, if you told me, "Hey, I'm bringing you a sandwich," and you came to me—

TRAVIS: That's the same argument!

JASON: This is my whole point, it's semantics. It's stupid semantics, but everybody knows, if you talk about a sandwich, you're not talking about a fucking hot dog. If you're talking about a straw, it has this end and this end.

TRAVIS: It has one hole.

JASON: No, this end and this end. You look at it, there's a hole right there at that end. You look at the bottom, there's a hole at that end. It doesn't matter that there's a connector in between. Is a door—you fucking walk through the door. Like if I open that door and then I open this door, now I'm just living in a fucking hole?

TRAVIS: Yeah.

JASON: No!! I'm living in a fucking house!! And that's an entrance and an exit and that's an entrance and an exit. That's two fucking holes!!

TRAVIS: There's one hole in a straw, Jason. You can look through it.

JASON: No, I don't care whatever your fucking scientist buddies come up with or whatever anybody looks up on Google.

TRAVIS: What scientist buddies? Yeah, because I hang out with a bunch of scientists.

JASON: All right, let's do this. You're in the middle of the straw . . .

TRAVIS: I'm in the middle of a hole. What do I got?

JASON: We make a big straw around you. Okay?

TRAVIS: Yeah.

JASON: You look up. You look to your left and your right. Are you seeing one hole or two holes?

I DON'T CARE WHATEVER YOUR FUCKING SCIENTIST BUDDIES COME UP WITH OR WHATEVER ANYBODY LOOKS UP ON GOOGLE.

WHAT SCIENTIST BUDDIES? YEAH, BECAUSE I HANG OUT WITH A BUNCH OF SCIENTISTS.

TRAVIS: Look to my left, look to my right. Like, "Oh my God, I'm in a hole . . ."

JASON: No.

TRAVIS: "How did I get in the hole?"

JASON: This is preposterous.

TRAVIS: That's crazy!

JASON: If you're in a cave, you're in a cave and it's got multiple exits, are those all just one hole?

TRAVIS: I'm going to look around and be like, "I'm in a cave. This is crazy."

JASON: Listen . . .

TRAVIS: I'm not going to think that there's a hole at the end of the cave. I mean,

---

a cave is different than a hole. That's why an ant farm is different than a fucking hole.

JASON: This is the problem with these, these are stupid questions.

TRAVIS: Jason, there's no dumb questions. Moving on to the next question.

JASON: A taco's a sandwich!! A fucking burrito's a sandwich!!

TRAVIS: No, a taco can't be a sandwich.

JASON: I'm just saying, this is where you go into these semantics. Everybody knows what a fucking sandwich is. Everybody knows what a hot dog is. It's not a fucking . . . if you ask for a sandwich and somebody brought you a hot dog, you'd be fucking like, "What the fuck is this? I asked for a sandwich."

TRAVIS: Is a burger a sandwich?

JASON: I think a burger is a burger. I don't get into the semantics of it. I'm not going to go into, is it a sandwich? We all know a sandwich when we see one. That's a burger. A hot dog is a hot dog. I'm not going to go into "Well, what classification is it?" Or, "Hey, does this straw have one hole, two holes?" Like if it's a silly straw, does that count as one hole? I'm not getting into all this. It's got this end and this end, and both of those ends has a hole in it. I don't give a fuck what happens in the middle of it. Two holes.

TRAVIS: We've spent enough time on this . . .

If you could take away one rule in football and you could add one rule in football, what would they be?

92%er: @Emoryguy via X

TRAVIS: That is definitely not a dumb question. That is actually a very intriguing question.

JASON: Clearly the penalty that I would get rid of is offensive holding because it's an offensive lineman's nightmare.

TRAVIS: You can't get rid of that.

JASON: I sure can. It said, it asked in the prompt, it was very specific. If you could take away one rule in football, I would take away the one rule that makes my job infinitely harder. I would take away holding.

TRAVIS: What about defensive holding? You're going to keep defensive holding?

JASON: Of course. I don't care if it's fair or not, I just want my job to be easier.

TRAVIS: I thought we were talking about what will make the game better and more entertaining. That's what I thought.

JASON: All right, we can do it that way.

TRAVIS: I'm saying what's a bad rule? Taunting. We should be able to taunt. We're a professional organization. We should be able to taunt the other player. And I'm not talking about like—

JASON: What does that have to do with professional organization?

TRAVIS: Because when you're going through the ranks—like high school, college—you're still developing. I think at a younger age, it's not necessarily needed. But heck, if we're going that route, let everybody taunt. Who cares if you can't stop me? Don't get mad at me.

JASON: We have to have respect for your opponents.

TRAVIS: I've got great sportsmanship. What? I'll shake everybody's hand after the game.

JASON: Not if you're taunting. Is that sportsmanship?

TRAVIS: Just playing the game. What do you mean? I'm a respectful taunter. Me catching the ball makes you feel bad enough.

JASON: I'm trying to think of dumb rules. What's a rule that I don't like that exists?

TAUNTING. WE SHOULD BE ABLE TO TAUNT. WE'RE A PROFESSIONAL ORGANIZATION. WE SHOULD BE ABLE TO TAUNT THE OTHER PLAYER.

TRAVIS: Can't take your helmet off.

JASON: See, you want to get rid of all the rules that aren't going to affect the game, though.

TRAVIS: What do you mean? Taunting definitely affects the game. It's a fifteen-yard penalty.

JASON: Well, if it gets called, but removing the penalty is not going to make the game change.

TRAVIS: I think it will make it way more entertaining when you get to what I'm going to say for my other rule.

JASON: What's your other rule?

TRAVIS: I want to bring in . . .

JASON: What do you want to bring in?

TRAVIS: One fight per game, hockey style. How electric would that be? Two heavyweights, O-line, D-line, just snap the helmets off. We get thirty seconds, just duke it out right here. Once we hit the ground, game's over, but—

JASON: Who's stopping it? The ref stops it once it hits the ground?

TRAVIS: Yeah, we might have to have bodyguards on the sidelines just for that one moment. You only get one player per team. This can't be a gang up like five on five. It's one on one. One on one. That's it.

JASON: You both take your helmets off, square up. Let's settle this.

TRAVIS: Let's settle this right now.

JASON: God damn, that would be exciting. I'm not gonna lie.

TRAVIS: It would be the first play of the game. Well, it would be like we did the first drive. Guys would just be like, all right, here we go.

JASON: Why was that grandfathered in the NHL, but for some reason no other sport allowed that to happen?

TRAVIS: I don't know, man, but fuck, I love going to hockey games for it. A bare-knuckle brawl, baby.

JASON: You barely ever see anybody get knocked out in those hockey brawls.

TRAVIS: It's hard to get a good lick on somebody. Especially if you know the good technique. If you know the technique, opposite shoulder, you got to extend. You can't let them get a full swing at you.

JASON: You grab the jersey. Once you have the jersey, you can control that shoulder, right? Yep.

TRAVIS: Until you can't.

JASON: Or you do the jersey over the head.

TRAVIS: Mighty Ducks style. Bash Bros.

JASON: There would be some vicious knockouts. I can't imagine. Are there weight classes? Are defensive linemen fighting linebackers? Like is there receiver versus D-line?

TRAVIS: Don't be barking up the wrong tree, dog.

JASON: Are you only allowed to fight with the guy that you're chirping with? Or can another guy come in? Like is this just going to turn into like 1980s hockey with enforcers?

TRAVIS: You're going to go get an enforcer.

JASON: We have our enforcer. You have their enforcer.

TRAVIS: Somebody's signing Mike Tyson. Come on, Mike. We're going to need you one play a game.

JASON: I would love to watch it. I'm not going to lie.

TRAVIS: Let's do it in the NFL, man. Let's make this game more exciting. Get the ratings up.

JASON: If we did it right now, who's the enforcer on the Chiefs?

TRAVIS: Oh, that's a good one. I'm going to go with Frank Clark, baby.

JASON: Frank Clark? Not Chris Jones? Yeah, he's got some hands.

TRAVIS: He's got them hands, baby.

JASON: He's a little bit light, though. Like, if he goes up against a bigger guy.

TRAVIS: He goes up against bigger guys all the time.

JASON: All right. I'm trying to think of who our enforcer would be.

TRAVIS: I might know who it is.

JASON: Who do you think it is?

TRAVIS: Number 62.

JASON: It's definitely not me. I ain't fighting nobody.

TRAVIS: You were the enforcer in Cleveland Heights. I know that.

JASON: Once upon a time, maybe, but not now. I'm too old for that.

TRAVIS: You were the LEL enforcer.

JASON: LEL enforcer.

TRAVIS: Lake Erie League, baby. Shout-out to the Lake Erie League.

JASON: I feel like it would have to be either Jordan Mailata just on pure size or Linval Joseph.

TRAVIS: Big Fletch [Fletcher Cox].

JASON: Fletch could do it too. I feel like Linval Joseph. He got a hell of a reach. He's like three forty, three thirty.

TRAVIS: It's a big dude.

JASON: Big man. Yeah, we got some guys.

TRAVIS: Good for you. I cannot keep this conversation going without mentioning Trey Smith being an enforcer.

JASON: Oh yeah.

TRAVIS: I cannot forget about 65, baby. Six-five is definitely laying down the law.

JASON: Some of those videos of him going at it with different guys, whether it's [Jeffery] Simmons over there in Tennessee. I love the way the guy plays the game. I really do. So that makes sense.

TRAVIS: Me too. I love that fucking guy. Shout-out to Trey. He's definitely our enforcer too.

What do you got? You didn't name your two holding, offensive holding and then what else? Which one would you add? What rule would you add? I always think of how baseball always tries to make the game more offensive. They do stuff to try and add to the hits and everything, wind the baseballs a little tighter.

JASON: I would change the motioning rules. You should be able to be more chaotic on offense, but presnap. I don't think you should have to be set.

TRAVIS: Canadian style?

JASON: I like the Canadian rules on motions.

TRAVIS: Canadian Football League.

JASON: Where you can get a full-on running start. Or also just having multiple people in motion. It's already such an advantage for the offense when that happens. The fact that like the defense doesn't have to be set, but the offense has to be set, it's just a dumb rule.

Is that not fair? Like the defense, they can be moving all over the place. They can be hiding everything. But the offense, you have to be set. If two guys go in motion, they both have to come back to a complete stop for a second. You know what I mean? There's some really cool things that could happen from an offensive structure if you allowed, if you change those motioning laws.

TRAVIS: We got both of our deals. It's pretty solid.

JASON: The only thing I would do is go back to the old rules of overtime.

TRAVIS: You don't like the new rules?

JASON: No. It's like, oh, well, the coin toss, we got a possession and you didn't. Oh, well, now we get the position back and then you're going to go back and score again. It's like a never-ending thing.

It's like, dude, listen, the game is tied. Next point wins. Stop complaining. Life isn't fair sometimes. You lose a coin toss. You got to go play some defense. I don't know what you want me to say.

TRAVIS: I've been on both sides of this.

JASON: So have I!

TRAVIS: You had four quarters before that overtime to put a drive together to put up points that you should have put up points on. You can't wait.

JASON: Yeah, I'm out. I'm out on these. It's ridiculous.

TRAVIS: I think another cool rule, just me personally, would be pretty sweet. If you got one double pass either per game or per half.

JASON: Double pass, meaning?

TRAVIS: Meaning you could throw a slant, a forward pass, and the guy that caught the slant could throw a fade on the other side of the ball, on the other side of the field. How electric would that be? Yeah, you want to talk about touchdowns, baby. And turnovers.

JASON: That would be interesting to see how that changed the game. So basically, for one play, well, you want to just throw one double pass, or would it just be for one play, there's no rules as to—forward, lateral, and stuff? However you want to move this ball around, move the ball around.

TRAVIS: That would be crazy. You could forward, lateral, just like basketball, fast break style. You're just three men weaving in.

JASON: You're playing rugby, essentially, right? Oh, no, you can't throw the ball forward in rugby either. You can only throw it backward.

TRAVIS: The lateral rule is different, though. I think as long as the ball is behind you after you pitch it, like once you pitch it, as long as the ball is behind you when the guy catches it.

JASON: So you can throw it forward and outrun it?

TRAVIS: Yeah. It has to be wherever, like if you're on the 4-yard line, the guy who's catching it can't catch it on the 5. It has to be on like the 3.

JASON: I remember seeing a clip and Russell Wilson was scrambling and threw a ball. It was a lateral, but when you paid attention to the hashes, it actually moved forward like a half yard. And I remember just being like, "Guys, what the fuck are we talking about?"

TRAVIS: It's behind them.

JASON: This is going to happen once a season. Maybe this is not a big deal. They overdo it sometimes with this stuff. Because of replay, there's such an emphasis that everything has to be perfect and nailed and like all of this stuff is going to be subjective to a certain extent of what's happening live on the field. I don't know, whatever.

TRAVIS: You do know. You just said it.

JASON: What used to be a catch was clear. It was like the clearest rule in the world. And then Dez Bryant had to go across and have this one moment [in the 2014 NFC Divisional Playoff game between the Dallas Cowboys and the Green Bay Packers]. And now we've been changing what is a catch for like the last ten years. And now nobody knows what a catch is basically. It's a little bit clearer now, but it was really unclear, like two years ago.

TRAVIS: It was the same thing as the quarterback, the tuck rule. The QB forward pass, in the pocket, is the elbow coming forward? Has he tucked it yet? They've been changing that thing back and forth since [Tom] Brady and the Raiders went at it.

JASON: Have they? They made the wrong call in that playoff game. That was clearly a fumble, right?

TRAVIS: Not if you go by the rules.

JASON: No, by the rule back then it was a fumble. They had to change the rule, and then they changed it back, right?

TRAVIS: I think that's the situation.

JASON: I don't know. I can't remember. It looked like a fumble.

TRAVIS: Damn it. I hate when I can't remember. That was a great question. I enjoyed talking through that question, and hopefully the NFL allows fighting like hockey.

JASON: That would be a great rule change. I'm all for that. What happens at the end of the fight?

TRAVIS: Ooh, that's a good question. Do you get like a quarter removed? Five minutes in the box? Do we get a box in the NFL now? You get a penalty, you got to go to the box for a few plays?

JASON: A little NFL sin bin?

TRAVIS: That's a pretty good one to add.

JASON: I think that'd be good. Where would the box be at?

TRAVIS: End zones.

JASON: It has to be, right?

JASON

A LITTLE NFL SIN BIN?

TRAVIS: It's the most fucking rowdy.

JASON: Yes. You got to go sit in the end zone.

TRAVIS: In the stands too. There's got to be a glass box in the stands. You just get fucking rained on.

JASON: God, that'd be awesome.

If you could temporarily live in any board game Jumanji-style, like the movie it comes to life, which game would you choose?

92%er: Heathrbee via Threads

TRAVIS: I'm going to go ahead and say fucking Jumanji.

JASON: Yeah, I mean, Jumanji is pretty damn good. That'd be a fun one. I feel like I'm already living in Monopoly.

TRAVIS: Seriously!

JASON: I feel like we're already doing that.

TRAVIS: The older I got, the more I understood. Oh, wow. This is like the Life game.

JASON: Battleship would not be fun. What? Dude, I don't want to be in a freaking naval war, getting sunk.

TRAVIS: The thing is, is that Battleship is just a guessing game. There's no real strategy.

JASON: I don't want to live in it, though. I don't want to get sunk and then drown. That doesn't sound fun. I'm not going into Risk or Battleship.

TRAVIS: Life was a fun little board game.

JASON: I'm already doing that one. So I don't need to go there. Which ones would be fun to go to? You strike me as a guy that would love to go into Clue.

TRAVIS: I did love that fucking game growing up.

JASON: You love murder mysteries. You'd be all over trying to figure out who done it.

TRAVIS: Kylie killed Jason in the basement with the sword.

JASON: I know the girls would all prefer Candy Land. That's where they would want to go. I can't do that much candy. That's too much. I'm not going into Candy Land.

TRAVIS: I'm in on candy, but not like that.

JASON: Operation, I'm not operating on nobody or getting operated on.

TRAVIS: No, I really wasn't in on that one either. What other board games are there? What am I missing?

JASON: Checkers, chess.

TRAVIS: You can't be in that game, though.

JASON: Connect Four?

TRAVIS: No.

JASON: Hungry Hungry Hippos?

TRAVIS: No.

JASON: No.

TRAVIS: That's all I got. Yeah, I'm going with Jumanji, though, man.

JASON: Jumanji does sound like the most fun. I mean, they made a whole movie off it and then they made another movie off of it . . .

TRAVIS: Then they made another movie off of it . . .

JASON: There's a third one?

TRAVIS: I'm pretty sure there's three, yeah.

JASON: Wow.

TRAVIS: Am I mistaken? Are there only two?

JASON: Well, *Jumanji.*

TRAVIS: No, there's two.

JASON: Time out. *Jumanji*, though, isn't really a board game. What are we talking about? *Jumanji* is not an actual fucking board game.

TRAVIS: Yeah, but it's a Jumanji-style.

JASON: It might be now, but you can't say *Jumanji* is a board game.

TRAVIS: Yeah, that's a good point. I'm just thinking I would want to fucking relive that movie.

JASON: It's a great movie.

TRAVIS: Yeah, I guess Monopoly.

JASON: Is there anything we're missing?

TRAVIS: Probably.

JASON: Yeah, I guess Candy Land. I mean, it just sounds like the most magical place. It doesn't seem like it's too serious. So we're just going to have some fun.

TRAVIS: Nice. Can't die. Yeah, I'm just here to enjoy it.

What Olympic sport would you be good at? Can't be a sport you've ever played before.

92%er: s_haack

TRAVIS: Me and Jason have kind of been on this, and I've never actually played it, but we both kind of been in on, "Hey dude, let's just go and see if we're good." I'm drawing a blank on what it's called.

JASON: Talkin' 'bout curling?

TRAVIS: Yes. Let's just go and see how good we are at curling.

JASON: Yeah. I mean, listen, we're good at cornhole. We're good at beer pong.

TRAVIS: Bocce ball.

JASON: We're good at bocce. I was just playing bocce ball on the beach.

TRAVIS: We just got to see, because somethin' 'bout that touch.

JASON: I'm a good sweeper.

TRAVIS: Jason's just— *[mimicking him sweeping]*

JASON: I mean, I don't sweep often, but when I do it, it's good.

TRAVIS: You're tactical. You're tactical and you're brilliant. And we'd be really good at being cheeky with it.

JASON: We're tacticians.

TRAVIS: That's what I'm saying.

JASON: It's the way we're wired. We're sneaky.

TRAVIS: We get our understanding of angles and speed and I just feel like we'd kill it.

JASON
WE'RE TACTICIANS.

TRAVIS
THAT'S WHAT I'M SAYING.

JASON
IT'S THE WAY WE'RE WIRED. WE'RE SNEAKY.

JASON: We'd also be good at a two-man bobsled.

TRAVIS: Neither one of us can drive. I don't know if that's the best.

JASON: We got the Ed Kelce genes there. Just jerky.

TRAVIS: Just jerky.

JASON: Dude, I can't get in a car with Dad. "Are you not feeling what you're doing to this fucking thing right now? I'm getting seasick. How the fuck am I getting seasick?"

TRAVIS: You got to love how everyone looks at their family members driving, man.

JASON: But then I found out I'm the same way. Kylie thinks I drive the exact same way as Pop.

TRAVIS: I know for a fact everybody thinks that I drive like that. So it's whatever. I'm going to say curling.

JASON: I'll double down on curling.

TRAVIS: Let's get out on the ice, man.

JASON: So we're winter Olympics guys.

TRAVIS: Oh, a hundred percent. Keep me out of the heat.

JASON: Do we have a Summer Olympic [sport] that we would maybe be good at? There's a list here Brandon has compiled. Why do Summer Olympics just seem so much harder? Handball. We used to play handball in the backyard with Dad.

TRAVIS: We were a big handball family.

JASON: Technically, you need to play handball in a racquetball court, I think.

But I think we could do that. We could do handball. Though maybe not, my elbow's shot.

TRAVIS: Yeah, my shoulder. I don't have the arms anymore. I can't even throw a fucking baseball.

JASON: We're too heavy for equestrian.

TRAVIS: Yeah.

JASON: I mean, Kylie could do field hockey. Fencing?

TRAVIS: No.

JASON: Just looks weird. Beach volleyball. I'd be the setter.

TRAVIS: I don't know.

JASON: I think we could do beach volleyball.

TRAVIS: Dude, it's shoulders again. I'm not doing this.

JASON: Badminton? You ever seen those guys play badminton? How hard they hit that shit?

TRAVIS: Dude, you gotta be fuckin' skilled to see that shit.

JASON: That shit's fun to watch. I like watching badminton.

TRAVIS: Badminton's good.

JASON: High-level badminton play? Exciting. Let me tell you.

TRAVIS: Dude, we're going to have to watch the Summer Olympics.

JASON: Dude, artistic swimming, also known as synchronized swimming?

TRAVIS: You're a male cadet.

JASON: We can both swim. I was a male cadet at high school.

TRAVIS: I'm elegant.

JASON: Trav is a knowingly great dancer. And he can swim, so he could probably answer.

TRAVIS: "Knowingly great dancer" is such a wild statement.

JASON: No, it's not. It's a very well-known fact.

TRAVIS: Because I fucking do dumbass dances in the end zone, I'm a "knowingly great dancer"?

JASON: No, you know why. Because you're a great dancer. I think we'd make a hell of an artistic swimming team.

TRAVIS: All right. I'm down. Synchronized swimming. All right. It's one of my favorite movie intros of all time. Which one am I thinking of?

JASON: What movie? I know, I can picture the scene.

TRAVIS: Dude, legendary. He does the whole dancing in the street with people that are just minding their business.

JASON: Is it *Austin Powers*?

TRAVIS: YES!

JASON: Yeah!

TRAVIS: *[singing the theme song]* Just watch the opening to *Austin Powers*, and you'll fucking know what I'm talking about. It's great.

JASON: I got it now, I'm with you.

What is the difference between a jamoke and a jabroni? And can they be used interchangeably?

92%er: @myrachristina via X

JASON: I'm going to defer this to our resident expert and potentially expert of the world on the differences between "jamoke" and "jabroni" in Travis Kelce, as he's the only one I really know that's still using "jamoke." And he's clearly—

outside of The Rock—the most prominent person still using "jabroni." So if there's anybody that needs to answer this question, it's Travis Kelce.

TRAVIS: I use them interchangeably.

JASON: Okay.

TRAVIS: I just feel like "jamoke" is more like stupidity, "jabroni" is more like you're just a fucking loser.

JASON: That's what I was going to say.

TRAVIS: And I call myself both at times.

JASON: I think they mean the same thing.

TRAVIS: I call myself a jabroni and a jamoke more than I call anybody else.

JASON: For sure. But I think what you're saying is they both mean the same thing, but the context and the way they're used is usually different. "Jamoke" is usually used as either a self-deprecation or a lighthearted way of calling somebody stupid or a fool, right? Whereas "jabroni" is the same meaning, but you're kind of taking a dig at somebody more than "jamoke" is.

TRAVIS: One hundred percent.

JASON: It's more like an offensive, like you're trying to get at him a little bit more with "jabroni." Is that accurate?

TRAVIS: You hit it right on the head, so you didn't even need to defer that to me.

JASON: Well, I've heard you use them a lot, so I've kind of picked up on the context.

TRAVIS: Yeah, you're a fucking jabroni.

If you could choose any two sports to combine together (a la *BASEketball*), which two sports would you choose and why?

92%er: Lizofh_town via Club 92

TRAVIS: Reading this before, I immediately thought of one of my favorite movie sport scenes of all time, which is *Happy Gilmore* when Bob Barker beats the shit out of Happy.

JASON: It's a great movie. Solid movie.

TRAVIS: Seeing that in real life would be unbelievable. So I'm going to say boxing and golf.

JASON: I feel like we kinda did—

TRAVIS: Oh, we did do something like this, didn't we?

JASON: I would combine NASCAR and gymnastics.

TRAVIS: NASCAR and gymnastics? This has just become Evel Knievel or some shit.

JASON: They got to do the floor mat while you got to jump over the car while it's moving full speed.

TRAVIS: This sounds like Nitro Circus.

JASON: And you got to land it. You got to stick the landing. The car does like a bunch of flips and sticks it.

TRAVIS: They have this actually with monster trucks.

JASON: It sounds like monster trucks, but with regular cars.

TRAVIS: Dude, some of the things that these monster trucks are doing when they fly in the air.

JASON: Yeah, monster trucks are cooler.

TRAVIS: They are unbelievable.

JASON: Yeah, you're right. That already exists. It's called monster trucks.

TRAVIS: I saw a clip of somebody playing hockey and football. It was like football rules on the ice.

JASON: Ooh, I did see that. I mean, it was nice. It's *incredibly* dangerous. Can you imagine trying to tackle somebody and drag somebody down with skates attached to their feet?

TRAVIS: I don't think they had skates on. It was just football on ice and hockey equipment.

JASON: Oh, they were just running? Good point. Well, either way, terrible idea, because I don't know if people know this, but ice is harder than concrete.

TRAVIS: Hard as fuck.

JASON: It sucks getting hit down on ice. How about swimming and sharpshooting?

TRAVIS: So what would be the weapon? It would just be like a bow, like a crossbow?

JASON: You got to tread water while you're shooting sporting clays or something like that.

TRAVIS: Okay.

JASON: What's a good thing to combine with swimming?

TRAVIS: Have you seen the little torpedo soccer game that they play underwater?

JASON: No, that sounds exciting though.

TRAVIS: Remember the little rubber torpedoes that you used to throw underwater and you would see it like a submarine, like you could pass it underneath water to your friend?

JASON: I don't, but it sounds great.

TRAVIS: We used to play this all the time.

JASON: Oh, you're talking about the little ones that you would throw under there?

TRAVIS: They turned that into an actual game where you could fucking tackle people and hold them underwater.

JASON: It sounds like my kind of game.

TRAVIS: It is your kind of game.

JASON: What about lacrosse and polo? Because it doesn't make sense that those guys on horseback are hitting that ball all the way on the ground. Just play lacrosse on horseback. I think that would be a legit game.

TRAVIS: I'm kinda in on that. That would be legit. Did you know you have to have like four horses per person?

JASON: Per person? Why do you have to have four per person?

TRAVIS: I don't know. I just heard that. So I thought I'd throw it out there and see if you want to call bullshit on it.

JASON: I'm callin' bullshit on it. I don't really know why you would need that. Four per person?

TRAVIS: Endurance, maybe? I don't know.

JASON: Oh, maybe that's it. They gotta sub the horse in and out?

TRAVIS: Yeah.

JASON: That's my kind of sport. Let's let the horse get tired. I'll just sit on top and have all the fun. I kind of like that.

TRAVIS: Dude, do you remember WhirlyBall?

JASON: WhirlyBall, yes.

TRAVIS: It was bumper cars and lacrosse.

JASON: Yes! Dude, that was a great game. That's what I'm talking about.

TRAVIS: It's in Columbus, Ohio, for those of you that are around the Columbus area. WhirlyBall. Make sure you guys go check it out.

JASON: Are we sure that they invented that? I mean, I know it's in that area, but it's got to be elsewhere.

TRAVIS: Dude, I've been trying to find it everywhere else and I can't find it anywhere.

JASON: What are we doing? Let's open up some WhirlyBall spots.

TRAVIS: They're so fucking fun. I went there like four or five years ago.

JASON: How about skydiving? Is skydiving a sport?

TRAVIS: We can make it.

JASON: Skydiving and slam dunk contests. That'd be pretty incredible.

TRAVIS: I don't know how—like are the hoops in the air or where are they?

JASON: I mean, it's to be determined. It depends on how many points you want. You can go all the way to the ground, but it's a lot harder to get it in there. You got hoops at different levels.

TRAVIS: What about skydiving and track? Like who can get to land first?

JASON: See, now you're thinking. Who can get to the ground first?

TRAVIS: Who's gonna pull their parachute last?

JASON: You're basically playing chicken. I think it's a fantastic idea. It'd be very fun to bet on.

TRAVIS: This is electric, is what it is.

JASON: Travis Pastrana would be dead.

TRAVIS: Nah, you can't kill that guy.

JASON: There's no way he's backing down. He'd figure it out, though. It'd be some other idiot that would freaking die.

TRAVIS: Travis Pastrana doesn't die. All right. Yeah, knock on wood. Shout-out to all the cool Travises out there that made my name cool.

JASON: The only person in the world with more lives than a cat.

If Jason had to push Travis or his wife over a cliff, who would he choose? He must choose one.

92%er: @MrJDANGER1 via X

JASON: Here's my answer. And tell me if I'm correct. Should I answer first? Or do you want to answer first?

TRAVIS: This question is for you.

JASON: Okay. I'm pushing Travis over . . .

TRAVIS: Nice.

JASON: . . . BECAUSE he would tell me to push him over the cliff.

TRAVIS: One hundred percent.

JASON: BAM, BABY!

TRAVIS: Don't you fucking push Kylie off of a fucking cliff. Are you kidding me? I'll be just fine. I'll tuck and roll. I'll flank away to safety. I don't know how the fuck I'll do it. I'll fucking sprawl out like a flying squirrel or some shit. I'll be fine.

JASON: Should we keep reimagining this question?

TRAVIS: No, I think you answered it.

JASON: If you had to push me or Mom over a cliff, who would you choose?

TRAVIS: God damn it, Jason.

JASON: You must choose one. Don't skirt the question, Travis.

TRAVIS: Mom's like seventy. You have kids that need to be raised. God damn it.

JASON: Don't skirt the question, Travis. You gotta choose one.

TRAVIS: I'm gonna choose Mom because you would want me to push Mom.

JASON: Oh my God.

TRAVIS: Oh man. I wouldn't push either of you, I'd jump off.

JASON: When I first read this question, I thought the exact same thing. Like, I'd just jump off of the cliff. But I don't think it works like that. I think the answer, dude, you gotta push me. This is the code of being a man. When the lifeboats are getting loaded, the women and children go first.

TRAVIS: Yeah, touché.

JASON: You gotta push me. But I think Mom would jump off. She's not on here to vouch, but I know that if it was me versus any of my siblings, I'm jumping off the fucking cliff. You don't even gotta push me. Well, unless that's not allowed, then I'll tell you to push me. I'll give you the nod. For future reference, if we're ever in this scenario. If I just go like this. *[wide eyes, nodding]* Push me. Right off the cliff.

TRAVIS: You're fucking hilarious. Nice. Just in case we ever get caught in that scenario.

JASON: Just in case we ever get caught in this ridiculous hypothetical situation. Push me.

Do you think rugby players have a chance in the NFL?

92%er: @sper40 via YouTube

JASON: We actually do have a former rugby player that is playing in the NFL, Jordan Mailata. But unless you're six-nine, 380 pounds, I would say that the chances are limited.

TRAVIS: It's just a different game.

JASON: It's a much different game. I think people keep comparing 'em.

TRAVIS: There's one common skill set and that's—

JASON: Quarterback sneaks?

TRAVIS: Toughness.

JASON: Oh, sorry. Toughness.

TRAVIS: You might be able to get a kicker. There's a few Australian punters in the league that I know of. They've all started off being footy guys.

JASON: Kicker would be the best chance, or punter. And then if you're an enormously skilled athlete, of course there's a chance you could play in the NFL. That is always on the table. But as a blanket statement, I'm going to say no. Rugby is more . . . the energy system is like soccer. There's not like stoppages, and it's not as violent, if that's the right word to say. It's not as high-impact. Is that fair?

TRAVIS: I can't say that to be true. I think it's still very much as physical as football is. I just don't think there's as much skill in rugby, respectively.

JASON: Well, I mean, I guess I play offensive line, which requires zero skill, but I could certainly see a tight end being the case. The physicality of the two sports is different. In rugby you're not wearing pads, so each hit is going to hurt a little bit more. You see them bleeding all the time. They're bleeding, they're bandaged up, it looks gnarly, their fingers are torn up, their ears are cut up.

TRAVIS: I want to go watch a game right now.

JASON: I know. I love watching. But the NFL, because of the pads, the collisions are just much more forceful.

TRAVIS: Yeah.

JASON: But you don't see as much of the typically gruesome features that you'll see in rugby. And I got to say, you're going to be hard-pressed to tell me the rugby players are not—

TRAVIS: Tougher?

JASON: Who is tougher? Conventional metrics. I'm probably going rugby. Those dudes are pretty tough.

TRAVIS: They don't wear pads, dude. But I will say this—not a lot of them are three hundred pounds.

JASON: It's just a different level. Would you rather get punched in the face ten times or would you rather a Nissan sedan run you over once? That's kind of the different levels of physicality.

TRAVIS: You're going to have to explain that one, big head. Which one's which?

JASON: Rugby is like you're getting punched in the face ten times. You're not going to have pads on, somebody's going to punch you physically, it's going to hurt. It's going to be brutal. You got to be a tough guy to take a hit. Right? The Nissan sedan, you're going to wear pads, but it's going to run you over. Then that's like a football collision.

TRAVIS: I will say this, people ask me all the time, "Do all the hits hurt?" It's just like, you know those Birds, the scooters that you get downtown?

YOU'RE GOING TO HAVE TO EXPLAIN THAT ONE, BIG HEAD.

JASON: Yeah.

TRAVIS: Those things probably go anywhere from fifteen to twenty miles per hour. You can get some of them up probably even faster than that. But imagine just taking that into the park and going across the park and then getting it up to seventeen miles per hour and then having somebody clothesline you. That's football essentially.

JASON: When they've done the impact studies, they compare it to car collisions.

TRAVIS: Not questioning the toughness and how physically demanding rugby is. Could football players play rugby? There's probably a lot of guys in the NFL that would not sign up for that gig.

JASON: No, definitely not.

TRAVIS: But the Kelce boys will.

JASON: I'd for sure do it. I think that might be fun.

TRAVIS: Looks like a fucking blast. I'd flank like a motherfucker. I'd be the one drop-kicking it and running to go get it.

JASON: Yeah, that's a good move. Solid move.

TRAVIS: I lateraled it last week.

JASON: We already know about my quarterback sneak skills. We'd be scrumming it up.

TRAVIS: Who knows? Maybe we'll see a rugby player one of these days become an NFL superstar like Jordan Mailata did.

Would you rather have muffins for hands or sweat mayo?

92%er: @stack4ttack via X

TRAVIS: I'd rather have muffins for hands. You make me sweat mayo, I'm going to fucking be throwing up my entire life.

JASON: I mean, it's an easy one. Sweat mayo. I need opposable thumbs. You got to grab things. What the fuck are you going to do with muffins for hands? Except eat them.

TRAVIS: Fuck. You're right. I just can't buy into mayo.

JASON: Just stay in the AC, baby. Then you don't sweat.

TRAVIS: I sweat in the AC, too.

JASON: That's a good point.

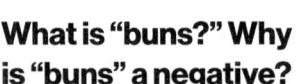

What is "buns?" Why is "buns" a negative?

92%er: Nina Grekin via email

TRAVIS: Like a buns number? Yeah, well, it's ass is what it is.

JASON: It's cheeks.

TRAVIS: Booty cheeks. There's nothing good that comes out of your booty. All right? It's all exit. It's all waste back there.

JASON: So I actually took a study of language class in college, Nina, and I'm going to explain to you why language evolves and changes. So the way this statement could be reworded would be, instead of it being a *buns* number, it's a *shit* number, right? So it's a shit number, meaning it's a bad number. Well, where does shit come from? Well, shit comes from ass.

TRAVIS: Comes from your booty.

JASON: So it's an ass number. So it's a shit number. It's an ass number. It's a bad number. Oh, what else is ass? It's cheeks.

TRAVIS: Cheeks is another one. "That shit is cheeks."

JASON: It's an ass number. What else is cheeks? Buns. So you just kind of got to follow the order of operations. What are buns referring to? In this context, it's calling the number shit.

TRAVIS: It's a whack number.

JASON: Yeah. It's stupid. It's bad.

NEW DUMB QUESTION

What are three books you guys would like to have if you were stranded on a desert island?

92%er: @ohkeilaknows via X

JASON: What's the longest book that we know? Some encyclopedia, to have plenty of toilet paper.

TRAVIS: Okay.

JASON: All right. Two more.

TRAVIS: Yes. Gotta have three.

JASON: A survival book ... like any book that would help me survive on this island for any period of time.

TRAVIS: Tom Clancy.

JASON: I do not think Tom Clancy is gonna be any help to you on the desert island. Like, *Escaping off a Desert Island for Dummies*.

TRAVIS: *How to Build a Raft*.

JASON: Yeah, there's gotta be some book that's been written by somebody that is like *How to Get off of This Insanely Terrible Predicament*.

TRAVIS: Dude.

JASON: I'm not fucking reading *Harry Potter* on the deserted island.

TRAVIS: I'll go with a *How to Make a Raft* book. And then I'd do something that I could try and perfect on the island. Does this island have golf?

JASON: It's a deserted island!

TRAVIS: ... that could have golf on it.

JASON: No, it couldn't. Golf courses do not exist in nature. Are you saying it used to contain civilization and is now deserted?

TRAVIS: Was there once energy on this island? Are there batteries? Are there solar panels?

JASON: Travis, you are not making ...

TRAVIS: Bro, being deserted on a deserted island back in the fifties is way different than nowadays. Everyone's bought up all the islands.

JASON: Yeah.

TRAVIS: There's no island unbought right now. So, there could be, like, treasures everywhere ...

14

Science

If you had to swap your legs with the legs of any other animal, which animal would you choose?

92%er: @BritSlo via X

TRAVIS: This is a dumb-ass question. What do we wanna . . . what do we . . . are we . . . how are we . . . yeah.

JASON: So we're swapping legs. Tell you which one I'm definitely not doing. Them knock-kneed-ass ostriches. Fucking going backwards and stuff. Why's it that kind of knee? Are we going for power, or are we going for length? Are we going for speed?

TRAVIS: Them motherfuckers are fast though.

JASON: So you want fast?

TRAVIS: Are we only doing two legs? Two-legged animals?

JASON: I guess.

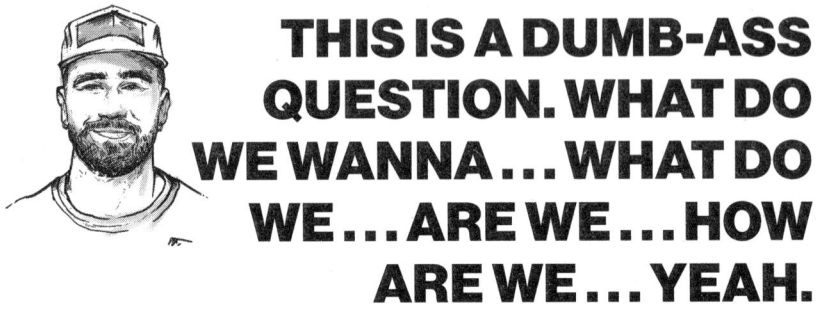

THIS IS A DUMB-ASS QUESTION. WHAT DO WE WANNA...WHAT DO WE...ARE WE...HOW ARE WE...YEAH.

TRAVIS: Four-legged animals?

JASON: If we swap with a four-legged animal . . .

TRAVIS: Do we lose our arms?

JASON: These are great questions. Let's say for the sake of this question, we're just swapping our two legs with two-ish similar legs of a four-legged creature, if you choose a four-legged creature. Meaning we still have arms.

TRAVIS: What the *fuck* did you just say?

JASON: Like if we go with a four-legged animal, we really still only have two legs, but they're kind of in the mold of the four legs.

TRAVIS: Who are you going with, dude?

JASON: I don't know. I don't know if I want power, if I want length, if I want speed, if I want strength. But like I said, definitely not ostrich. I mean, you can't go with something like a dachshund with them little short stumpy things.

TRAVIS: No, you can't, definitely not a dachshund. Little wiener dog? No way.

JASON: Or do we want to say you get the number of legs? Because then if you're a spider, you get eight of 'em.

TRAVIS: That's not an animal.

JASON

INSECTS ARE ANIMALS, TRAVIS. PART OF THE ANIMAL KINGDOM. IT'S GOT ITS OWN, LIKE, SECTION.

JASON: Insects are animals, Travis. Part of the animal kingdom. It's got its own, like, section.

TRAVIS: God damn it, Jason.

JASON: Is that true or am I wrong? Animals, insects . . . maybe you're right. Well, you just saw a rhino. Rhinos got some powerful legs. You saw that in person. You felt that girth in them legs.

TRAVIS: Listen, I saw how bouncy that thing was.

JASON: It was bouncy?

TRAVIS: Dude, that thing was like . . . *[bounding from side to side]*

JASON: All right. So you got tall ones. If you wanted to be tall, you go giraffe, right? I mean, you'd be a pretty good basketball player with some giraffe legs.

TRAVIS: [Victor] Wembanyama.

JASON: He has giraffe tendencies. If his neck was a little bit longer . . .

TRAVIS: You can't tell me that dude wasn't made in a fucking lab over there in France.

JASON: Is he from France?

TRAVIS: Yep.

TRAVIS: Lab-grown diamonds. That's lab-grown fucking—

JASON: Human.

TRAVIS: —NBA player.

JASON: Listen, it's not far off. Let's be honest.

TRAVIS: Can't wait till I fucking make one.

JASON: Don't do this. Do not give any of these other conspiracy theorists anything else to latch on to, please.

So you want speed. You got cheetah, right?

TRAVIS: Jason, *what are you going with*?

JASON: I'm trying to talk this out to see where I'm going. I don't know yet. Just got to ask a question.

TRAVIS: Give me—

JASON: You're not offering anything.

TRAVIS: You're right.

JASON: You've said no animals.

TRAVIS: Because I still don't know— if we're counting four-legged animals in this.

JASON: We're counting all-legged animals. You can go millipede. How about that?

TRAVIS: All right. But if I lose my hands, I don't want to fucking do it.

JASON: You still have hands. You still have hands.

TRAVIS: So if I switch with a four-legged animal, now I just look like one of the mythological creatures, like the man on top of a horse. Boom.

JASON: No, I think if you have four legs, no. If you have four legs . . .

TRAVIS: Man on top of the horse. Give me that guy.

JASON: If you pick a four-legged animal, you're only taking the hind legs. Your front legs are . . . your front . . .

TRAVIS: Okay, so only hind legs.

JASON: But if you pick more than a four-legged animal, like an eight-legged animal or a centipede, then you have to give up your hands. Don't worry, it makes sense. You'll get a kangaroo jumping out the gym.

TRAVIS: Yeah, but you need a tail. I'm telling you, saw that thing live the other day? You need a tail. So if you don't get the tail with it, it's fucking pointless.

JASON: Has there ever been a tailless kangaroo?

TRAVIS: Nope. Never.

JASON: One of them has never got chopped off or something?

TRAVIS: Maybe.

JASON: They do balance on that thing.

TRAVIS: Dude, they do a lot with that thing.

JASON: I guess if I'm picking any animal's legs in this scenario, I'm gonna go with elephant.

TRAVIS: Elephant legs?

JASON: It's got height. It's got power. They're pretty fast. What other animals got better legs than an elephant?

TRAVIS: I'm not gonna lie, I might go ostrich, dude. Those things are fast, man.

JASON: The knees go backwards, Travis. You're just asking for something bad to happen.

TRAVIS: No, no.

JASON: Taking some bird legs? You're gonna come at this thing with some bird legs?

TRAVIS: Dude, not just some bird legs. One of the fastest fucking birds you've ever seen in your life.

JASON: It's fast because it's light though. You're not light. Those legs will crumple under the weight of Travis Kelce.

TRAVIS: Fuck. Yeah, you're right.

JASON: That knee direction only makes sense on something that's got minimal mass up top.

TRAVIS: Feathers?

JASON: How much does an ostrich weigh?

TRAVIS: We're getting too dumb.

JASON: We're going too dumb. We're going too dumb with it.

TRAVIS: Yeah, we're going too far dumb.

TRAVIS

WE'RE GETTING TOO DUMB.

JASON

WE'RE GOING TOO DUMB. WE'RE GOING TOO DUMB WITH IT.

TRAVIS

YEAH, WE'RE GOING TOO FAR DUMB.

JASON: *[looking up ostrich facts]* I mean, yeah, I guess you're in the range. One hundred forty to 320 pounds is a male ostrich. If you took out your legs, you're probably in that range, but you're on the lower end of that range if you take away your lower-half mass and put some little-ass ostrich legs on you.

TRAVIS: Give me the man on top of the horse.

JASON: No, we just said that . . . you don't get to have—Minotaurs are not—you don't get that . . . you're like—

TRAVIS: I'll do horse legs, then. I do horse legs.

JASON: You know what you are? You remember the movie *Hercules*?

TRAVIS: Give me Clydesdales.

JASON: Okay, no take-backsies! No take-backs! He took horse. You are like the mythological creature in *Hercules*. The one that had the little legs.

TRAVIS: You're talking about a Pegasus?

JASON: No, it's not a Pegasus. I forget what it's called.

INTERN BRANDON: *[offscreen]* Not a Pegasus. He had goat legs.

TRAVIS: He had goat legs. No, those weren't horse legs.

JASON: But same thing.

TRAVIS: What?

JASON: No, you're the same thing, but you got horse legs.

TRAVIS: I gotta be short and stumpy like that?

JASON: No, you're still tall because it's horse legs, not goat legs, but you only get the two.

TRAVIS: So who'd you go with? You went with elephant legs?

JASON: Elephant. Should have gone crab legs. Would have had some armor.

TRAVIS: This was fucking so dumb.

Could 100 guys beat one gorilla?

92%er: @bdfghklnpquvwxy via X

JASON: Are we allowed to use tools? 'Cause I can beat a gorilla by myself if I got the biggest gun. Be over *real* quick, right? So I think we're talking about hand-to-hand combat, I'm guessing.

TRAVIS: Yeah, I think we're just talking hand-to-hand.

JASON: Gorilla don't scare me if I got a big-ass Magnum fucking . . . whatever. You can tell I know a lot of guns.

TRAVIS: But what are we talking here? What's a win? Is a win death?

JASON: Yeah, you're fighting to the death. That's what a win is when you're fighting a gorilla.

TRAVIS: How do you . . . ?

JASON: How do you kill it?

TRAVIS: That's what I'm saying.

JASON: That's my thing!

TRAVIS: How do you kill a gorilla?

JASON: You're gonna need a tool. You can't kill a gorilla with your hands. What are you gonna do, choke it out? I mean, it's gonna be tough.

TRAVIS: That's gonna be a tough sell right there.

JASON: I think a hundred guys could do it 'cause the gorilla would get tired. But he's gonna go through about ninety-eight of 'em.

TRAVIS: Somebody's getting *fucked up*. I think a hundred guys would beat one gorilla. Everybody just got to be *dedicated to the shit*. The shit is, you're gonna get fucked up if you're one of the first people to go at this gorilla.

JASON: I think one of the reasons these questions are terrible is because humans don't fight hand to hand. You go back to looking at people back in the day, everybody's using tools. I'm gonna pick up a big-ass rock. I'm not gonna go fight this gorilla with my hands. I'm gonna let you distract him. I'm gonna stand in the tree and then when he's not looking, I'm gonna drop a boulder on his head. We're not fighting fair. That's how human beings fight. Right?

TRAVIS: I'm with you.

JASON
IF YOU TRY AND GO FIGHT A GORILLA WITH YOUR BARE HANDS, *YOU WILL DIE.*

JASON: If you're smart, if you want to survive. I'm gonna sharpen a stick and then poke that big motherfucker and not have to go and fight it with my hands. In which case, it's gonna be a lot less than a hundred guys. Might be one guy, if you got the right tool. But yeah, if you try and go fight a gorilla with your bare hands, *you will die.*

TRAVIS: I'm not fucking with that.

JASON: It's too strong. It's too powerful. I don't even know how you would kill it. How would you kill a gorilla?

TRAVIS: Dude, what? I don't know. You're not choking it out.

JASON: You try and hold it down. Would twenty people jump on it, just to pin it down? But even that, I don't think that's going to work.

TRAVIS: I think they're twenty times stronger than us. That's why it's a dumb question.

If you could make one of your body parts detachable, which would it be and why?

92%er: @fclsegd via X

TRAVIS: Detachable?

JASON: It's a very weird question. I'll wait for you to answer first.

TRAVIS: I don't know. Maybe my ears so I wouldn't have to hear people.

JASON: That's what I was thinking too.

TRAVIS: Nose? Because I think smells can be . . .

JASON: You're going senses.

TRAVIS: I think smells can be a little more . . .

JASON: There's some mayonnaise in the area. You don't want to have to smell that.

TRAVIS: I'm not trying to smell that shit. I'm going senses though. I'm going ears or nose.

JASON: Ears or nose. Ears would be nice. You're trying to get some shut-eye, just take your ears off. Sleep tight.

TRAVIS: Then you're never waking up. You have to get something that shakes the room or something.

JASON: All right. I'm just going to throw it out there . . .

[Long pause. Travis looks suspicious.]

JASON: I mean, if we're being honest, it usually just gets in the way.

TRAVIS: Jason.

JASON: I mean, it's an inconvenient appendage at times. I mean, listen, I'm very happy I have one.

TRAVIS: The ball and chain?

JASON: I feel like it's a one . . .

TRAVIS: No, there's two different—

JASON: It's a one-stop shop. I think it's all the same appendage.

TRAVIS: I don't think that's how it works.

JASON: No? It just gets in the way sometimes. Like if you're running, you got to think there'd be less friction without that in between your legs trying to play sports, right?

TRAVIS: No, I don't think about it. It doesn't bother me at all.

JASON: And then I feel, let's just be honest, if you can detach it, that means you could probably attach an upgraded one. You know what I mean? You could go bigger. Assuming it's like a universal connection point, I could attach another one.

TRAVIS: You're a fucking psychopath, man. I was waiting for you to make it make sense. And you never disappoint.

JASON: Is it like the iPhone charger where they went to all just USB-C, like we're going to one standard connection?

TRAVIS: You're hilarious.

JASON: "You'd lose your dick if it wasn't attached" is what Dad used to tell us.

TRAVIS: He used to tell me that all the fucking time.

JASON: Maybe that's why I thought of this immediately. You're right, Dad. I don't want it to be detachable because I would definitely lose that motherfucker. You're right. We don't want that to be detachable. This has got to stay on. I'm not responsible enough to have a detachable dick.

JASON

I'M NOT RESPONSIBLE ENOUGH TO HAVE A DETACHABLE DICK.

What was the first person to milk a cow trying to do?

92%er: Mercyrjacob via Instagram

JASON: I think they were trying to milk a cow.

TRAVIS: Yeah. I don't . . . what came first, the chicken or the egg?

JASON: The milk or the cow?

TRAVIS: I don't fucking know.

JASON: I think the milk came second. The cow had to be there for the milk to come out of the cow.

TRAVIS: It's true.

JASON: All I'm saying is I don't know, dude, why would there be anything else expected other than the milk coming out of the cow? This isn't the question, like, how did the first person figure out that smoking weed got you high? They saw calves drinking out of the fucking cow's udders, they knew that there was milk in the udder, and they just milked the fucking cow and drank the milk. But there's not, like, a question mark here.

TRAVIS: We might have our first dumb question.

JASON: Yeah.

TRAVIS: This might be the first one, feels like.

TRAVIS
WE MIGHT HAVE OUR FIRST DUMB QUESTION.

JASON
YEAH.

TRAVIS
THIS MIGHT BE THE FIRST ONE, FEELS LIKE.

If you could redesign one thing about the human body, what would you change and how would it improve?

92%er: Rude-Product2975 via Reddit

TRAVIS: Like . . . let my feet be the same as my hands.

JASON: So you want to be essentially a monkey?

TRAVIS: I just want to be able to grab things—make my toes longer so I can grab as much as I grab with my hands.

JASON: You're literally describing a chimpanzee. I mean, I guess yes, we can also steal from the animal kingdom. We're not chimps. And we potentially never were related to them. Although, I think most scientific data would suggest some type of common ancestor, unless you don't believe in evolution, which . . . okay, let's not go down this rabbit hole . . .

TRAVIS: We already went down one. Let's keep going down all of them.

JASON: I would make everybody's arteries better so that you could eat bullshit food and not have to worry about getting congestive heart issues or hypertension or anything like that. I would get rid of ramifications for eating delicious food.

TRAVIS: God damn. I'm gonna eat some delicious food right after this.

JASON: I would make our sense of smell better. Be able to smell like a dog. Dogs' sense of smell is so strong, they can smell diseases and illnesses and things on people that not even human technology can detect at certain times. Even before there was a COVID test, dogs could actually detect it at a higher rate. And even once they had the test, dogs were a higher-percentage chance of knowing whether you had COVID or not, and they could smell it on you. I think that'd be dope. And I think it would make human beings a lot better.

NEW DUMB QUESTION

If a woman woke up in the man's body for one day, what would be the most unexpected experience that she didn't already anticipate?

JASON: How stupid you are.

TRAVIS: Like, "Why aren't the neurons firing? Why is it taking so long to process things? Things that don't matter."

JASON: "My brain is not functioning right now."

TRAVIS: "Why am I buffering?" My brain has never buffered.

JASON: Yeah. It's still loading at all times.

TRAVIS: It's still loading the whole day. You go to sleep and think about all the shit you need to do tomorrow just to wake up and load again.

JASON: "Why am I not listening to what anybody tells me? I'm just preoccupied in my own thoughts."

TRAVIS: Thinking about my next meal.

JASON: I get by thinking about what I want for lunch or that new truck that just came out. How much toilet paper gets stuck in your ass hair when you wipe?

TRAVIS: Jesus.

JASON: Well, I think that's pretty ubiquitous, right? I feel like every man's got to deal with a portion of that. We just have hairy assholes. Doesn't every man have a hairy asshole? Brandon, do you have a hairy asshole?

INTERN BRANDON: Sure do. End of chapter.

15

Special Guest NDQs

Would you still want to be six foot eight if you were bad at sports? (*feat. Jayson Tatum*)

92%er: Elise_jost

JAYSON TATUM: Oh, uh—

JASON: It's a great question. A lot of inconveniences come with that height.

JAYSON TATUM: How like—how bad?

TRAVIS: Like, you're not even getting picked at the rec.

JASON: Yeah. Last pick in dodgeball.

JAYSON TATUM: Yeah, I love me at six-eight. I ain't gonna lie.

JASON: Fair enough.

TRAVIS: I respect it.

JASON: The not being able to find shoes that fit is an inconvenience I can deal with for being six-eight. I love it. For sure. If you had to play an entire game wearing flip-flops, how many points are you realistically dropping?

TRAVIS: You still finding a way to get some space?

JAYSON TATUM: Flip-flops? I mean, I just sprained my ankle last night wearing basketball shoes . . .

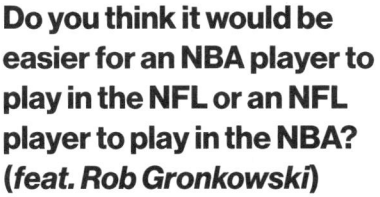

Do you think it would be easier for an NBA player to play in the NFL or an NFL player to play in the NBA? *(feat. Rob Gronkowski)*

ROB GRONKOWSKI: Oh man. I like that question, but it's going to be easier for an NFL player to play in the NBA.

JASON: What?!

TRAVIS: BOOOOOOOOOOM! Thank you, Rob!

JASON: No! You tight ends, man. You guys are ridiculous. What makes you say that?

ROB GRONKOWSKI: The hitting aspect. And also what makes me say it is watching Draymond Green play tight end.

JASON: Everybody thinks of this.

ROB GRONKOWSKI: And I lost my mind.

TRAVIS: It was like his first day!

ROB GRONKOWSKI: I don't care. I was confused.

JASON: He went outside hands. I don't know what he's thinking.

ROB GRONKOWSKI: I was like, what the heck? Yeah, I mean, you can throw us in. I seen Mike Evans play basketball. And I was like, man, this dude is legit.

TRAVIS: He's a dog.

ROB GRONKOWSKI: He could definitely play. I was like, if he focused on that, he's got NBA talent. It was impressive. And a lot of receivers have that type of talent. But also you can throw someone in there like a tight end or something and you can just have a role for them as a role player.

TRAVIS: That was my argument. Might not be a superstar, but we could find roles for sure . . .

ROB GRONKOWSKI: Exactly.

JASON: I disagree with both. But you know what . . . ?

TRAVIS: Take that right in the fucking face, Jason.

TRAVIS
TAKE THAT RIGHT IN THE FUCKING FACE, JASON.

JASON: I'm getting ganged up on by tight ends. All right. We've also debated signing babies on the show, whether that's acceptable or not to sign a baby. I got a feeling you've got, you have a crazy story. What is the craziest thing you've signed?

ROB GRONKOWSKI: I actually never signed a baby, thinking about it. And that would be a little crazy, like their skin. They're absorbing everything in the baby.

TRAVIS: That's what I'm saying, Rob, thank you!

ROB GRONKOWSKI: You're putting that ink on the baby and it's going right through the skin, like right through their pores.

TRAVIS: I don't want to do that to them.

JASON: They pick up stuff off the floor and shove it in their mouth every single day.

TRAVIS: The Sharpie box has a warning that says keep away from eyes and mouth.

JASON: I don't think it does. I want to see that warning.

TRAVIS: I pulled that out of my ass.

ROB GRONKOWSKI: It has to.

TRAVIS: Makes sense.

ROB GRONKOWSKI: It doesn't. If it doesn't, it better now. But I've signed some crazy things, like some dollar bills and stuff, shoes, phone cases, phones. These twelve-year-old kids, they all want it on their forearm. That is weird. And then I did some people's foreheads as well, too. You know, twelve-year-old kids are like, "Sign my forehead, sign my forehead!" And then they show it off. And then their parents are shaking their head like, "Oh my gosh, not your forehead."

JASON: But they probably secretly want it too.

ROB GRONKOWSKI: Yeah.

JASON: And they're like, "You shouldn't have done that. Let's get a picture."

TRAVIS: "I'm next. I'm next. Sign mine next." Dude, that's electric.

JASON: I love it.

TRAVIS: One last question, brother. We're all vets in the game here. If there was any advice that you would give your younger self to make your game that much better, is there any one thing?

ROB GRONKOWSKI: I would give myself two advices. Coach [Bill] Belichick always told us this one, that the best answer is *no*. If I could go back, I would have definitely said no to probably half of the things that I did on the field and off the field, especially off the field. I mean, you got started at like twenty-two years old. You don't know how to say no to people or anything. You're not a grown man yet. You can get bullied over pretty easy. I can say no to anything now, but at that time, it's hard to say no and you'd be doing things just to please other people.

And then the other one would be to take care of yourself, to take care of your body. Like I said, if I could go back, I would definitely have started doing treatment on your body, getting body work done and all that, and learning how your body works functionally, instead of going out there and just trying to run at people every time. So take care of your body and learn how to say no.

TRAVIS: That's great advice. What about you, Jason? You haven't told us what you want to tell your younger self.

JASON: I think what I would tell my younger self is, just embrace people. I think when I was younger, I had a lot more rigid viewpoint of what I thought doing the right or wrong thing is or playing in the NFL was. I think as I've gotten older, I've learned to appreciate guys for who they are and what makes them unique and what makes them special. I think that might be partly like the Andy Reid mantra was: "Embrace your personalities." I think that that's probably the one thing I would say to my young self. Don't try and be anything, just freaking be yourself and be a baller and go play the game.

TRAVIS: Right on, baby.

How close are we to *The Terminator* becoming a real thing? (*feat. Arnold Schwarzenegger*)

ARNOLD SCHWARZENEGGER: I think we are very close. People ask me all the time, "How do you feel about AI?" I said I'm not as concerned about artificial intelligence as I am about basic stupidity.

JASON: Gosh, that was the best answer I could have ever heard.

ARNOLD SCHWARZENEGGER: Real-life stupidity worries me more than the AI.

JASON: That's fair. I mean, that's very fair.

Hypothetically, who would be a more successful athlete: Travis Barkley or Charles Kelce? (*feat. Charles Barkley*)

92%er: @Sethgillitzer via X

TRAVIS: This is hilarious. We've told the story about me wanting to be named Charles when I moved to the new city, Cleveland Heights, when I was five years old. My mother found out at the block party, I was telling everybody down the street that my name was Charles. You just told the story about how Travis Abernathy was one of your idols in the city you grew up in.

JASON: Man, I've got to ask you a few things. I watched that episode of *The Steam Room* with you guys. There's no way you actually wanted to be called Travis. You had to have made that up for the show, right?

CHARLES BARKLEY: No, not at all. What was really funny, the best player at my high school was a guy named Travis Abernathy. He was great from like junior high. So everybody loved Travis. But I was named after my grandfather.

So when I started getting better at basketball, I said, "Mom, what do you think about me changing my name to Travis?" She says, "What the hell are you talking about?" I said, "Charles ain't going to get it done." She says, "That's your grandfather's name." And I said, "Yeah, and he's a nobody." That's a perfect example. But hey, Jason, that's one hundred percent true. I'm not just saying this because we had him on the podcast.

JASON: This is so crazy.

CHARLES BARKLEY: I've told a story on the show twenty-five times. I love the name Travis. It's just like, you got to be able to play some if you're named Travis.

JASON: Yeah, for sure. That's a bad-ass name for the most part.

CHARLES BARKLEY: It is!

JASON: Yeah, that's fair.

TRAVIS: All right, I'll take it.

JASON: What about Jason? You ever thought about Jason?

TRAVIS: Yeah, I was about to say, would there be any Jasons?

CHARLES BARKLEY: No.

JASON: Don't have the same ring to it.

CHARLES BARKLEY: It doesn't have the same ring to it.

JASON: Oh my God.

TRAVIS: Definitely not Jason Barkley.

JASON: I was about to say, who has a better career, Travis Barkley or Charles Kelce?

CHARLES BARKLEY: I think they'd both been pretty successful. I think you got a huge advantage on me because you actually play both sports. So either one of them will work. Like I told you, man, that one day I played football, I knew football was not for me.

JASON: Well, D-line wasn't for you.

CHARLES BARKLEY: I always joke around with my football friends. Like defensive line, offensive line, running back. You know, you really have to be all in.

TRAVIS: Impose your will.

CHARLES BARKLEY: As a running back, when you get that ball, you got them boys coming for your head.

TRAVIS: Listen, I'm a flanker. I'ma find my way.

CHARLES BARKLEY: You can get some off plays.

JASON: Oh yeah, if you're on the back side?

TRAVIS: The back side. Run a little fake.

CHARLES BARKLEY: Jason, you don't ever get an off play.

JASON: No off play. Unless, well, sometimes there's two, three techniques and I just get to sit in the hole and act like I'm doing something. I'll go help the guard maybe, but that's about the only thing I get. And usually now they figure out like, hey, let's spike one of these guys down and hit this guy. So now they're gonna give me that one-off.

CHARLES BARKLEY: So my football friends tell me the center's the smartest guy because you have to do all the protection.

TRAVIS: Oh yeah. You can't be a dummy.

JASON: We've talked about this, Chuck. I really think Travis and I, the way we think, we ended up going into the positions that suited us. My dad tells a story, we got the same Lego set as kids. And I followed the instructions like one by one and put this thing together piece by piece. Travis just looked at the box and put the thing together. You know what I mean?

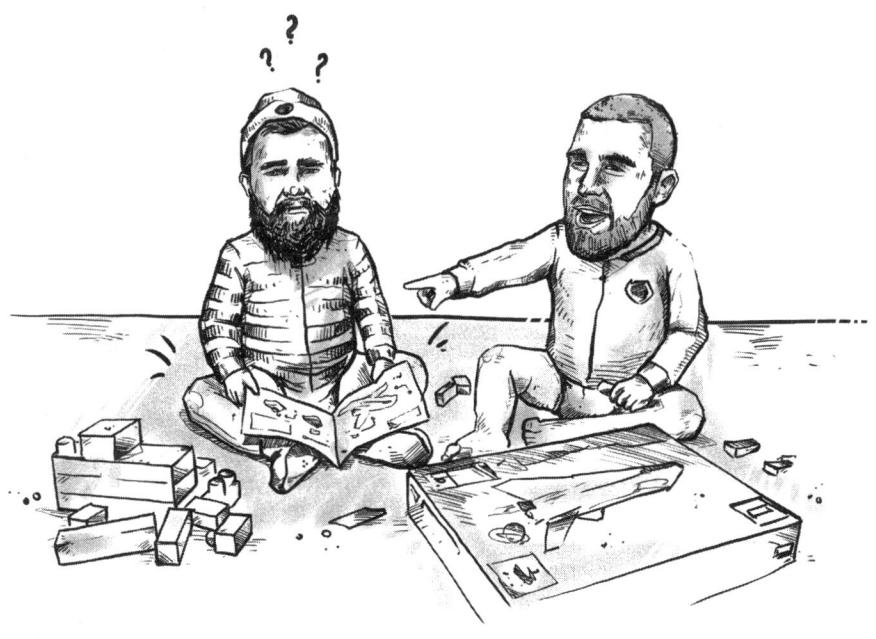

TRAVIS: Had a few extra pieces at the end that I probably shouldn't have had, you know what I mean? Missed a few steps, but that thing looked like the box.

JASON: Well, for years my dad was like "Travis is smarter than Jason, because he put that Lego set together *without* the instructions." But what I'm saying is I'm very analytical thinking, and I think it helps being a center. My brother is very creative, and he thinks kind of similar to an artist, where he's just got great spatial awareness. He is one of the smartest people I've been around.

And to be a center, you have to be able to understand the ins and outs of the play and make calls and do all these things that are structured. But I don't have the ability to freelance the way Trav does and the way a lot of guys that are premier either basketball players or receivers or quarterbacks—quite frankly, you watch Pat Mahomes, probably the best freelancing athlete I've ever seen.

TRAVIS: You gotta have a little bit of both.

What is your Mount Rushmore of summer activities, like at a barbecue? (*feat. Alejandro Villanueva*)

92%er: @barcelonababy12 via X

ALEJANDRO VILLANUEVA: At a barbecue, that's a very American concept. So I'm not—

JASON: You guys don't barbecue in Spain?

ALEJANDRO VILLANUEVA: No, no, there's not as much barbecue.

JASON: There's no shrimp on the barbie?

ALEJANDRO VILLANUEVA: No, the concept of the Fourth of July, taking a weekend off to go back to work in your summer job, I mean, Europeans take June, July, August off.

JASON: You just told me how excited you were to celebrate Fourth of July over in Spain.

ALEJANDRO VILLANUEVA: Yeah, yeah . . .

JASON: You got to have a barbecue over in Spain.

ALEJANDRO VILLANUEVA: I like to barbecue.

JASON: You like cornhole?

ALEJANDRO VILLANUEVA: Cornhole. Yep.

JASON: Okay.

ALEJANDRO VILLANUEVA: Spikeball.

JASON: Spikeball?

ALEJANDRO VILLANUEVA: I would put spikeball above anything else.

JASON: Really?

ALEJANDRO VILLANUEVA: I'm a huge spikeball guy.

JASON: What's the strategy of spikeball? I can't really understand it.

ALEJANDRO VILLANUEVA: It's the serve.

TRAVIS: You've never played?

ALEJANDRO VILLANUEVA: It's the serve. Everything is in the serve.

JASON: It's a lot of movement for a big fellow.

ALEJANDRO VILLANUEVA: No no no no no. I played spikeball and I was bigger than you. Yeah, spikeball is the funnest game in the world. Behind Ping-Pong, maybe. Ping-Pong is the best.

JASON: I like pickleball more than Ping-Pong.

ALEJANDRO VILLANUEVA: I like to be the barbecuer, first of all. I like to wear sandals.

JASON: Do you wear an apron?

ALEJANDRO VILLANUEVA: No, shirtless, duh.

JASON: Tongs?

ALEJANDRO VILLANUEVA: Spatula.

JASON: Spatula.

ALEJANDRO VILLANUEVA: Burgers. So I like to be the guy on the grill.

JASON: Do you like barbecue sauce?

ALEJANDRO VILLANUEVA: No.

JASON: So what do you put on your meats?

ALEJANDRO VILLANUEVA: Ketchup. Is that barbecue sauce?

JASON: No, I mean, well, Kansas City–based barbecue sauce is based on ketchup.

ALEJANDRO VILLANUEVA: Kansas City, now I got to go to Kansas City. Burger is cheese, burger, ketchup, buns.

JASON: Do you ever make ribs?

ALEJANDRO VILLANUEVA: I'm thinking about like an easy, simple barbecue. You want to talk about smoking something? You want to talk about like smoking a pig and now, okay, yeah, smoking a pig for sure.

JASON: So Mount Rushmore is?

ALEJANDRO VILLANUEVA: Spikeball, cornhole, barbecue, man.

JASON: We're missing one more. Like, the pool?

ALEJANDRO VILLANUEVA: I can shoot pool, yeah.

TRAVIS: No, not billiards.

JASON: Jumping in the pool.

ALEJANDRO VILLANUEVA: Oh, being in the pool? Yeah, I guess. I mean, shotgunning beers. Can we put shotgunning beers?

JASON: I'll put that on my Rushmore.

ALEJANDRO VILLANUEVA: Put shotgunning beers.

JASON: All right. Is it before spikeball or does spikeball beat shotgunning beers?

ALEJANDRO VILLANUEVA: Oh, these are not dumb questions. These are incredibly complicated questions.

JASON: Yeah.

ALEJANDRO VILLANUEVA: I have to win at spikeball. I have to be the king.

JASON: I got to try this spikeball thing.

ALEJANDRO VILLANUEVA: One hundred percent spikeball.

TRAVIS: I can't believe you haven't got it.

JASON: I think I've played it.

ALEJANDRO VILLANUEVA: We used to play it in the locker room. My teammate was Chase Claypool. Amazing athletic range. And we used to play during the COVID year, which is the funnest year in NFL history. We used to play spikeball for hours before practice. Hours.

JASON: What's the strategy to spikeball?

ALEJANDRO VILLANUEVA: The serve.

JASON: I thought the serve had to be nice and easy.

ALEJANDRO VILLANUEVA: No no no. Obviously that's number one. But then if you make the serve too easy, the other team is going to score right away. You have to play game theory. You have to threaten to make a really hard serve. And then do it like a little lay. So then they're like really far away. They can't make it. The serve is ninety percent of spikeball. And psychology. Meaning you have to intimidate your teammates, your opposing team.

JASON: How do you intimidate in spikeball?

ALEJANDRO VILLANUEVA: Dude, personal stuff.

TRAVIS: Aggressive spike.

JASON: Oh, wow. So you're trash-talking.

TRAVIS: Yeah.

ALEJANDRO VILLANUEVA: Personal. You go personal.

JASON: What's the best way to get in somebody's head trash-talking?

ALEJANDRO VILLANUEVA: I'll talk about—

JASON: Girlfriends, wives, kids.

ALEJANDRO VILLANUEVA: All the above. Whatever makes them insecure. You keep trying until you find it.

JASON: Alrighty. Well, dude, you're the best.

ALEJANDRO VILLANUEVA: No, you're the best.

TRAVIS: Dude, the most interesting man in the world.

ALEJANDRO VILLANUEVA: There's no such thing.

TRAVIS: No, there is. And you're him.

JASON: It's insane. I've never sat down with you and not been thoroughly enthralled.

ALEJANDRO VILLANUEVA: That's just because I'm a great bullshitter.

JASON: Well, you speak four other languages.

ALEJANDRO VILLANUEVA: Did a whole bunch of things. Every person is interesting. Equally as interesting.

JASON: I don't know about equally.

Could an average person gain one yard on a rushing play in the NFL? (*feat. Saquon Barkley*)

92%er: @VinkIsaac via X

SAQUON BARKLEY: Yeah.

TRAVIS: The average person?! Look at Jets Jake right now.

JASON: Jets Jake, come on camera so we can see what you look like.

SAQUON BARKLEY: I feel like I got to say yes now or I'm just dissing him, right?

TRAVIS: There's no hard feelings here. He's a Jets guy himself as well.

SAQUON BARKLEY: Do you play any ball back in your day?

JETS JAKE: No.

TRAVIS: There we go.

SAQUON BARKLEY: If you had to run a forty right now—under six seconds?

JETS JAKE: No chance.

SAQUON BARKLEY: No chance. So you're just not helping the cause at all.

JETS JAKE: Yeah, not at all.

TRAVIS: How's your vision?

JETS JAKE: Twenty-twenty.

TRAVIS: Twenty-twenty vision. That's a start.

SAQUON BARKLEY: Actually, I got to say, there's a game I had against the New York Jets. I had thirteen carries and one rushing yard.

JASON: Holyyy cow.

SAQUON BARKLEY: And I would say I'm a pretty good running back.

TRAVIS: At least you got one.

SAQUON BARKLEY: Soooo . . . you're probably not getting it.

JETS JAKE: Yep.

SAQUON BARKLEY: Yeah, average person is probably not getting one yard.

TRAVIS: Aaaand he's out. All right.

SAQUON BARKLEY: I had to think that one through.

JASON: I think about it sometimes, because like if a guard and a tackle destroy a double team, anybody could *probably* get a yard. But you got to think about how long it's going to take them to get to the hole. And how fast everything changes, right? If the average guy's Jets Jake.

SAQUON BARKLEY: If it's outside zone, no shot.

TRAVIS: Was that a shot? My bad, Jake. I love you. You're above average in my heart.

JASON: Above-average person.

SAQUON BARKLEY: That's what matters.

What NFL players should be in the WWE after retirement? (*feat. Chris Jones*)

92%er: @M_B57 via X

TRAVIS: You got anybody off the top of your head that you think would be perfect for a showman role in the WWE?

CHRIS JONES: George Kittle, man. I can see him.

JASON: That's the first one I think of too.

TRAVIS: Kittle's already whooping ass.

CHRIS JONES: Yeah, I can see Kittle doin' it.

TRAVIS: He was on *WrestleMania* this past year in Dallas, I believe.

CHRIS JONES: Yeah, it's very fitting for him.

TRAVIS: Kittle, for sure. I'll tell you what, DK Metcalf—

JASON: He definitely looks the part.

TRAVIS: He's ready to just jump off the top rope and fucking stunner somebody.

CHRIS JONES: His body's like a mannequin doll. Like it's crazy.

JASON: It's like hard plastic.

TRAVIS: I think it was the steroid era of growing up in the nineties where it looked like every single wrestler was just the biggest, strongest human being in the fucking world.

JASON: Well, that's one hundred percent what it was.

CHRIS JONES: Absolutely.

TRAVIS: I don't know if they're doing that quite as much now.

JASON: Chris, I got to ask you this. Where did your nickname "Stone Cold" Jones come from? Do you know? Did it just start happening or . . . ?

CHRIS JONES: Actually, Dave Grutman from Miami and I had this Instagram handle. It was like The Chris Jones, 96, MSU . . . he was like, we got to change it.

TRAVIS: Your typical one, yeah.

JASON: We got to make this unique.

CHRIS JONES: And he was like, "Stone Cold Jones." And I was like, "All right." And then everybody just started calling me Stone Cold. I was a huge wrestling fan.

JASON: Was Stone Cold always your go-to growing up?

CHRIS JONES: It was between him and The Rock. You know, I used to go to class and do the "Do you smeeellll . . . ?"

TRAVIS: ". . . what The Rock is cooking!" *[does The Rock's signature eyebrow move]*

CHRIS JONES: I used to do that in the middle of the class before they kicked me out, man.

TRAVIS: Hit him with that eyebrow?

CHRIS JONES: Ah bruh, I never could get it down, man.

TRAVIS: Too funny, man. Who's the tag team group? Like if there was a tag team in the league that would be in WWE?

CHRIS JONES: Tag team. Who's the good tag team?

TRAVIS: I'm saying you and Khalen Saunders, man.

CHRIS JONES: I was about to say me and Big Khalen, man.

TRAVIS: Would be the fucking best tag team. Talk about showmanship, athleticism. Oh my fucking goodness. The world doesn't know what they're missing.

CHRIS JONES: Khalen coming off the top ropes.

JASON: Doin' a stake down there in New Orleans.

TRAVIS: He's the only three-hundred-pound man I know that's out here just doing backflips in the middle of practice.

JASON: He is surprisingly athletic for how short and stubby—

CHRIS JONES: Three forty, bro. Three forty.

TRAVIS: Jesus, man. Out there moving.

JASON: I did not know he was that big.

TRAVIS: That shit's so impressive, man. Let alone running sideline to sideline and hawking shit. Shout-out to Sir Bink.

CHRIS JONES: Sir Bink. The Binkster.

About the Authors

Jason Kelce is one of the most beloved Philadelphia athletes of all time. As the Eagles' starting center, Jason helped bring the city its first-ever Super Bowl victory, holds the franchise record for most consecutive starts, and delivered an iconic parade speech that cemented his fan-favorite status. After a storied thirteen-year NFL career, Jason is a future lock for the Pro Football Hall of Fame and will be broadcasting as a part of *Monday Night Countdown* on ESPN. Outside of football, Jason and his wife, Kylie, have four daughters and are both major advocates for the Eagles Autism Foundation.

Travis Kelce aka The Big Yeti is an eleven-time Pro Bowler and three-time Super Bowl champ, having played thirteen seasons with the Kansas City Chiefs. One of the best to ever do it, Travis holds countless records, most recently becoming the Chiefs' all-time leading touchdown scorer. Off the field, Travis is building a significant media career with multiple projects under his belt and serves as the creative director for his lifestyle brand, Tru Kolors. He's also dedicated to his foundation 87 & Running, which helps empower disadvantaged youth by providing opportunities to explore their talents in business, STEM, and the arts.